P9-DFC-683

"This book is a feast for the senses. It is an invitation to see, hear, smell, taste and touch deeper spiritual realities through physical senses that are awake and alert to God in all of life. It gently but powerfully leads us into a life that is truly sacramental and enriched through the use of Scripture, personal stories and beautiful images."

Juliet Benner, spiritual director and author of *Contemplative Vision*

"With *Awaken Your Senses,* Brent Bill and Beth Booram have given us a superb resource for seeking the God of life through sensuous experience, a way of knowing that has been sadly neglected—and too often held suspect—by the church. How did a faith based on the claim that 'the Word became flesh' become so divorced from bodily, incarnate knowledge? Here is a beautiful book that will help us reclaim our bodies, our senses and our relationship with God."

Parker J. Palmer, author of *Let Your Life Speak*

"Amazingly, we become dull to something as extraordinary as life, and bored by someone as awesome as God. This book woke me up without beating me up, and gave me tangible, practical ways to savor the sacrament of life, to have genuine gratitude for my body and its senses, and to sink into the glory of God until I felt nothing but joy. Read this and be blessed."

James Bryan Smith, author of *The Good and Beautiful God*

"*Awaken Your Senses* invites us to notice God's movement in and around us. These pages grant us a permission to remember, and yet be more present through the conduit of our senses. This is the sort of resource that can help us keep a more rhymed company with God."

Randy D. Reese, author of *Spiritual Mentoring*

"*Awaken Your Senses* by J. Brent Bill and Beth A. Booram is a beautiful invitation to explore and embody the sacred sensual world. This delightful work invites us into a greater integration of head and heart, mind and spirit, through the use of mindful and creative exercises. It is a wonderful companion and guide for becoming more centered, present and aware in the midst of a busy life. What a joy to drink deep of *Awaken Your Senses*!"

Carrie Newcomer, Rounder recording artist, *The Geography of Light*

formatio

TRADITION. EXPERIENCE.
TRANSFORMATION.

Formatio books from InterVarsity Press follow the rich tradition of the church in the journey of spiritual formation. These books are not merely about being informed, but about being transformed by Christ and conformed to his image. Formatio stands in InterVarsity Press's evangelical publishing tradition by integrating God's Word with spiritual practice and by prompting readers to move from inward change to outward witness. InterVarsity Press uses the chambered nautilus for Formatio, a symbol of spiritual formation because of its continual spiral journey outward as it moves from its center. We believe that each of us is made with a deep desire to be in God's presence. Formatio books help us to fulfill our deepest desires and to become our true selves in light of God's grace.

AWAKEN YOUR SENSES

EXERCISES FOR EXPLORING THE WONDER OF GOD

J. Brent Bill & Beth A. Booram

JESSAMINE COUNTY PUBLIC LIBRARY
600 South Main Street
Nicholasville, KY 40356

IVP Books

An imprint of InterVarsity Press
Downers Grove, Illinois

InterVarsity Press
P.O. Box 1400, Downers Grove, IL 60515-1426
World Wide Web: www.ivpress.com
E-mail: email@ivpress.com

©2012 by J. Brent Bill and Beth A. Booram

All rights reserved. No part of this book may be reproduced in any form without written permission
from InterVarsity Press.

InterVarsity Press® is the book-publishing division of InterVarsity Christian Fellowship/USA®, a
movement of students and faculty active on campus at hundreds of universities, colleges and schools
of nursing in the United States of America, and a member movement of the International Fellowship
of Evangelical Students. For information about local and regional activities, write Public Relations
Dept., InterVarsity Christian Fellowship/USA, 6400 Schroeder Rd., P.O. Box 7895, Madison, WI
53707-7895, or visit the IVCF website at <www.intervarsity.org>.

Unless otherwise indicated, all Scripture quotations are taken from the Holy Bible, New Living
Translation, copyright ©1996, 2004. Used by permission of Tyndale House Publishers, Inc.,
Wheaton, Illinois 60189. All rights reserved.

While all stories in this book are true, some names and identifying information in this book have
been changed to protect the privacy of the individuals involved.

See p. 204 for additional permissions.

Cover design: Cindy Kiple
Interior design: Beth Hagenberg
Images: music notes: © dra_schwartz/iStockphoto
thorny stem: © Jivko Kazakov/iStockphoto
bitten pear: © John Clines/iStockphoto
old card: © Mike Bentley/iStockphoto
old paper with burnt edges: © Neil Sullivan/iStockphoto
rose on paper: © Roxana Gonzalez/iStockphoto
parrot on perch: Purestock/Getty Images

ISBN 978-0-8308-3560-7

Printed in the United States of America ∞

g green press INITIATIVE InterVarsity Press is committed to protecting the environment and to the responsible
use of natural resources. As a member of Green Press Initiative we use recycled paper
whenever possible. To learn more about the Green Press Initiative, visit <www
.greenpressinitiative.org>.

Library of Congress Cataloging-in-Publication Data

Bill, J. Brent, 1951-
    Awaken your senses: exercises for exploring the wonder of God / J.
Brent Bill and Beth A. Booram.
        p. cm.
    Includes bibliographical references (p.   )
    ISBN 978-0-8308-3560-7 (pbk.: alk. paper)
    1. Spiritual life—Christianity. 2. Senses and sensation—Religious
aspects—Christianity. I. Booram, Beth. II. Title.
    BV4509.5.B542 2011
    248—dc23
                                                                  2011032888

P	18	17	16	15	14	13	12	11	10	9	8	7	6	5	4	3	2	1
Y	27	26	25	24	23	22	21	20	19	18	17	16	15	14	13	12		

3 2530 60720 9069

MAY 0 8 2012

Brent's Dedication:

In memory and honor of Alan K. Garinger—writer, mentor,
inventor, educator, conservationist, rascal and my friend

Beth's Dedication:

In memory and honor of Margaret Mary Theising,
October 27, 1916–December 4, 2010: a woman who lived her
loves; the salt of the earth; a simple and true one; grandmother

CONTENTS

Prayer for Awakening the Senses

That in the elements of earth, sea, and sky

I may see your beauty,

That in wild winds, birdsong and silence

I may hear your beauty,

That in the body of another and the intermingling of relationship

I may touch your beauty,

That in the moisture of the earth and its flowering and fruiting

I may smell your beauty,

That in the flowing waters of springs and streams

I may taste your beauty.

These things I look for this day, O God,

These things I look for.

INTRODUCTION

Imagine awakening to the sound of the coffeemaker as it strains its final percolations and you smell the earthy aroma of its brew. You see dim light peeking from the edges of the shades at your bedroom windows. The feel of warm, soft blankets makes it hard to get out of bed. Once up, you look out the kitchen window, focusing your eyes on the early morning light, and feel greeted with hope, reminded that God is in new beginnings.

As you drive into work, you hear a siren behind you. The sound causes you to search in your rearview mirror for the lights. The alarm prompts you to pray—to pray for whoever might be hurt and for the safety of those you love. You feel your tightened grip on the steering wheel and think to relax, to concentrate on simply being and on trusting God with your life and your day.

During work, you notice things: the tone of stress in your boss's response to a question, the sparkle in your coworker's eyes as she describes her new romance, the firm handshake of a customer, the cool taste of water from a drinking fountain and the scent of a woman's perfume in the elevator. Life has so much depth and texture. You are alive to yourself and the world—curious and open to God's subtle invitations to pray, to love, to be. With each sensory prompt, you are learning to respond the way Jesus leads you.

Dinnertime and evening hours brim with sensual greetings. You prepare a meal with your family. The sounds of chopping vegetables and sizzling meat remind you that food is a gift. Everything you see, hear, touch, smell and taste turns your meal into an occasion—not only for your stomach but also for your heart.

Scrubbing greasy pots, rinsing soapy dishes and feeling the scald of hot water awaken you to the unending life cycle of soiling and cleansing, mess and order. Your thoughts turn to your own jumbled soul, to Christ, to his restoring work.

As you lie down to sleep, you notice your cold feet under the blankets, the taste of toothpaste in your mouth, the smell of dinner lingering in the air, the quiet of the house and the streak of moonlight beaming through the window. You feel thoughtful, grateful and pensive. Your heart turns to God, and you express your feelings of smallness and inadequacy. "What are mere mortals that you should think about them, human beings that you should care for them?" You entrust yourself to sleep and to God who does not slumber or sleep. Another day lived, hopefully more fully alive to God and yourself, alive to the beauty and suffering in life, to all its possibilities and cries for healing.

Have you ever longed to live this way—present to life, to God, throughout an entire day? It is possible. We each desire authentic spiritual experiences with God: real, moving, transforming engagements. The trouble is that's not how we have been taught to live our faith. Most of our teaching comes by way of sermons, books, Bible studies and other spiritual resources that instruct our thinking. Often, though, these resources miss our souls, the prime place of divine encounter. The book you are holding takes a different tack. Its purpose, simply put, is *to help more of you experience more of God.* How will we accomplish that? We're going to introduce you to spiritual practices that engage your whole person: both sides of your brain, all five senses and your body. In this way, you'll learn how to cultivate an experiential faith—one that trains you to be attentive to a self-disclosing God who reveals himself in each daily round of beauty.

HELPING MORE OF YOU

Your whole brain. Words are the primary form of communication we use to nurture our spiritual lives. They happen to be the language of the left brain. The left brain, which is the logical and concrete center of our thinking, uses words to understand and interpret experiences. However, the left brain cannot experience—God or anything else. The left brain takes meaning from our experiences; the right brain does the experiencing.

The right brain, the creative and intuitive center of our thinking, communicates through images, not words. By image, we mean anything you envision through one or more of your senses. For instance, if you walk into a room and recognize a familiar face (an image), you have just activated the right side of your brain through your sense of sight. When you smell the aroma of an apple pie and think "Grandma," you have just utilized your right brain through your sense of smell. When you listen to Vivaldi's *The Four Seasons* and it brings to mind the image of melting snow, you have heard the sound and processed it using the right side of your brain. Because the right brain does our experiencing, sensory spiritual practices that involve the right brain open us to a heightened perception and experience of God. Such exercises position our heart for divine encounter.

We need both sides of our brain in order to live and grow as a person of faith. In fact, neither side can do its job well without the other. Words provide content and information that are critical to faith formation, but words alone are not sufficient to create encounters with God that nurture wholeness. As Dr. Terry Wardle of Ashland Theological Seminary says, "We are over informed and under transformed." Why? Because we rely almost exclusively on word-oriented approaches that provide information about God but rarely facilitate engagement with God. We need to awaken both sides of our brain in order to experience God.

All five senses. Since we live so much out of our thinking, we often become divorced from our souls and bodies. We lose a sense of place, of rootedness in life. Using our senses helps us live in present time. That's important because the present is the only place we can experience God. We can't experience God while thinking of the past or planning the future. Neither exists right now. God can only be experienced in the reality of the present moment. When we attend to life with one or more of our senses, we immediately enter real time and awaken to the possibilities of God in it.

This idea of a sensuous spirituality, of attuning your senses to the sacred, may be new for you. It was for both of us. For Brent, it came into focus when a couple of friends teased him about the books he was writing. One of them said, "Gee, you have written about Quakers and sound [*Holy Silence*] and Quakers and sight [*Mind the Light*]— what are you going to do next? Quakers and smell?"

So Brent began to investigate the idea and found this quote by the founder of Quakerism, George Fox: "Now I was come up in spirit through the flaming sword into the paradise of God. All things were new, and all the creation gave another smell unto me than before, beyond what words can utter."

After discovering that quote, he found he couldn't let go of the idea of how our senses are involved in faith development. He then began looking through the Bible and found dozens of references to the physical senses in verses such as Psalm 34:8, "O *taste* and see that the LORD is good" (KJV); Matthew 5:8, "Blessed are the pure in heart: for they shall *see* God" (KJV); and 2 Corinthians 2:15, "For we are to God the pleasing *aroma* of Christ" (NIV, emphasis added for all).

At the same time Brent compiled this list, he and Beth met and began conversations about linking senses to spirituality. While we recognized the pure God-given sensory experiences of seeing a dramatic waterfall or smelling the delicate scent of a newborn grandchild as the gifts they are, we both discovered that thinking about our sensory experiences as windows into the life of the Spirit led us to opportunities of experiencing God in fresh ways. We acknowledged the senses and the experiences they bring to us as inherent blessings. But we also saw their potential to help us go deeper into our lives with God. With that in mind, we began a series of thirty-day experiments with each of the senses and posted our reflections on our blogs.

The body. One of the reasons for living as sensual beings is that it helps remind us that our bodies are carriers of spiritual truth. "Do you not know that your bodies are temples . . . ?" (1 Corinthians 6:19 NIV). A temple is a good place to go and learn about the Divine. Our body-temples have all sorts of things to teach us if we would just pay attention to the lessons they present. Too often, we live mostly in our thoughts—making lists and checking them twice—and spend too little time listening to what our bodies are saying. Yet Christians throughout history have known that our bodies have much to teach us.

Some faith traditions, more than others, model how to involve the body in worship and prayer as a way to express one's heart. And undeniably, any time we involve our bodies in kinesthetic response, we reinforce what we are feeling, thinking and doing. The actions involved in baptism, kneeling, anointing, lighting candles or coming to the altar for prayer all strengthen our internal attitudes through outward expression. But many of us have never been taught how to listen and respond spiritually to and with our bodies.

As an example of how our bodies can teach us, we invite you to try the following exercise. First, read the psalm below quietly to yourself.

You, God, are my God,
    earnestly I seek you;
I thirst for you,
    my whole being longs for you,
in a dry and parched land
    where there is no water.

I have seen you in the sanctuary
   and beheld your power and your glory.
Because your love is better than life,
   my lips will glorify you.
I will praise you as long as I live,
   and in your name I will lift up my hands.
I will be fully satisfied as with the richest of foods;
   with singing lips my mouth will praise you.
     (Psalm 63:1-5 NIV)

Now, breathe deeply. Relax your body and mind. Let your mind float over these words. Think about them slowly and gently. Savor each thought. As you do, ask yourself, *What posture might I adopt if I prayed this prayer aloud? Would I be prostrate? Upright, reaching toward heaven? Sitting in my chair with my palms upturned, ready to receive?* What does this prayer call your body to do? Then, if you dare, adopt that posture and say the prayer aloud.

EXPERIENCE

The point of the exercise above (and the ones that follow) is to help more of you—your whole brain, all five senses and your body—*experience* more of God. Since the left brain interprets our experience and the right brain does the experiencing through our senses, we have designed sensory exercises throughout this book and in the "Sensory Exercises" section at the back of the book to help position you for a divine encounter. We believe that such experiences are helpful to your spiritual formation, not as an end in themselves, but as a means to know God and live more deeply in him. Therefore, please don't gloss over these exercises or think of them as superfluous.

The same is true of the art pieces that open each section. Each was created to illustrate one of the senses in daily life, but they are also meant to be used as an art meditation. While we tend to think of art meditations as something we experience with great pieces of fine art hanging in marvelous museums or galleries, the art included here illustrates the holy among the daily—from the pure physical enjoyment of the juice from an orange to the reminder of how anticipation and thirst reflect our desire of a soul-satisfying experience of God.

So please take time to do the exercises and art meditations. They are integral in helping more of you *experience* more of God.

MORE OF GOD

Finally, in helping more of you experience *more of God,* we refer to the "wonder of God." God is the Life within life. Listen to the sentiments of author and theologian Richard Rohr: "All of life is sacramental; everything is a means of grace." The wonder of God encompasses the breadth of life, including episodes that surprise us and ones that confound us. Wonder is the awe we feel when we gaze up into the night sky, glimpse a hundred stars and sense the One who created them looking back at us. The wonder of God is also the mysterious ways of God that prompt us to ask, "I wonder where God is?" "I wonder why God didn't answer me?" "I wonder what God is doing?"

Through awakening your whole self, you will experience more of God as you live closer to reality and the facets of God that are difficult, mysterious and perplexing, as well as amazing, gracious and stunning. Wonder humbles us. Picture a small child, engrossed in the marvel of a ladybug or hushed into silence at the sound of a violin. We become like children when we are roused to the permeating presence of God in the witness of creation and the sacredness of an ordinary day. And it was Jesus who said, "I tell you the truth, unless you turn from your sins and become like little children, you will never get into the Kingdom of Heaven" (Matthew 18:3).

Awakening your senses to the wonder of God is what poet Caroline C. Graveson called becoming aware of the "daily round for beauty." She believed that God was in all beauty—natural and human-made. When things are "right"—be they serious or silly, humble or great—there is a fitness or correctness about them. They are pleasing to the eye, ear, nose, tongue, fingers and soul. Thus, a nursery rhyme can move us as deeply as a requiem by Mozart because God is in all beauty, both the simply amazing and the amazingly simple.

A SENSUOUS FAITH

Christianity is a sensuous faith. We often forget that. And some of us even get nervous thinking about it, probably because we confuse sensuous with sexual. While sensuousness is certainly part of God's gift of sexuality, sensuousness is so much more than sexuality. Especially when it comes to faith.

Our faith lives are filled with sensuous experiences. Some are solitary, as when we're alone in a devotional time and feel the thin pages of the Bible between our fingers. Others are in community as we gather around the smell of incense, sing hymns and meditate upon the cross—all these experiences and more (or less, depending on our tradition).

We invite you to join us in meeting Christ with all of your being—through the senses of touch, smell, taste, hearing and seeing. We want to help more of you experience more of God so that you come to love God with all of your heart, soul, mind and strength. This meeting will require something of you. It will require risk. You'll be stepping out of your comfort zone, stretching yourself through new and uncomfortable spiritual exercises. Growth and progress happen no other way. It will also take time. Please don't just read this book straight through. Practice it. Go as slow as you need, but do take time to participate in the experiences designed to help you encounter the Divine.

PAYING ATTENTION IN LOVE: A SPIRITUAL EXERCISE

We start using our senses to experience the presence of God around us when we learn to pay attention in love to our surroundings, the spots where we live. Though it is in God that "we live and move and have our being" (Acts 17:28 NIV), it is in very specific places like our homes, offices, farms, schools and the like where we actually live and move and *are* being. Take a few minutes now and look around.

- What do you see?
- What do you smell?
- What do you hear?
- What do you taste?
- What do you feel?

Grab a piece of paper (or a scrap of napkin, computer keyboard or journal) and write down your answers.

This is a simple step, but it is the first step in learning to pay attention. Seeing God at work and play around us, however, involves more than merely paying attention. Seeing God around us requires coupling our attention with love. When we look with love at something, we regard it. We notice the nature of it; we respect and appreciate it for what it is. We experience its "otherness" and see its intrinsic goodness and worth. For instance, the people we live and work with can become so familiar to us that we quit *really* seeing them. But when we stop and pay attention to them with love, we awaken to their distinctiveness—to the ways God has uniquely fashioned and formed them. We see the image of God in them. While we wish we could claim this concept as our invention, many people have written wisely and well about it before us. One of our favorites is a fellow named Belden Lane who teaches theology at Saint Louis University and has a deep interest in the sacred. Concerning paying attention in love, Lane writes:

Where can I *not* encounter the holy, has been the question of spiritual writers in every tradition and every age. "Whither shall I go from thy Spirit? Or whither shall I flee from thy presence?" asked the psalmist (139:7). Once our attention is brought to focus on the masked extraordinariness of things, we are hard put to discern the allegedly profane.

There are miracles all around us. They seem hidden because we do not see them, cloaked as they are in the ordinary. It takes the combination of attention and love to notice them. Loving attention sees the sadness in a friend's eyes, the flitting grace of a butterfly, the craftsmanship of a communion table, the early morning sparkle of dew across the lawn.

When we combine attention and love, we move to a new level of noticing. Love and attention give us a deep, clear look at God everywhere around us. So with the thought of paying attention in love, slow your breathing, quiet your mind and calm your heart. Now, take a fresh look around, with attention *and* love.

- What do you see?
- What do you smell?
- What do you hear?
- What do you taste?
- What do you feel?

When you're finished, write down your answers and compare them to what you wrote earlier. How are they similar? How are they different? How did you catch a glimpse or whiff or touch of the Divine?

By engaging your senses in ways like that above, you will awaken to the wonder of God all around you—a joyous, sensuous, spiritual awakening!

Part One

Taste

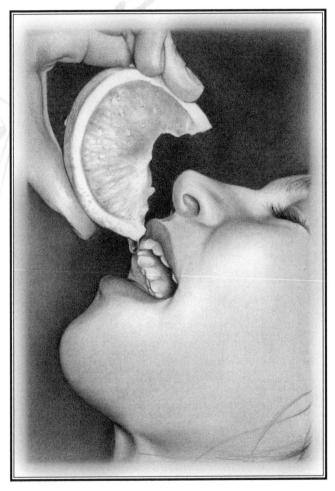

Art Reflection on Tasting

As you look at the illustration, take time to relax your body and mind. Breathe deeply. Think about the following questions slowly and gently as you look at this drawing. Savor each thought and each sensory experience that comes to you.

As you study this image of the woman tasting juice from an orange slice, where are your eyes drawn?

What do you notice about her experience of tasting the orange?

Did you see the drip of juice suspended from the orange slice? What happens when you focus on it?

How do you imagine the juice tasting to her? How would you describe the taste?

What would it feel like if you were holding the orange in your fingers? What would the texture be like?

If you were eating an orange like this, what other senses would be awakened? Describe them.

How does this image inspire you? What do you want to do or taste?

The artist titled this piece Thirsting for God *(Psalm 63:1). Have you ever thirsted for God in the way the woman in the drawing is thirsting for the drop from the orange?*

In what ways has a taste of God quenched your spiritual thirst?

1

INTRODUCTION

by Brent

Taste and see that the LORD is good.

PSALM 34:8

Often we taste the
granular body of wheat
(Think of the Grain that
was buried and died!)
and swallow together
the grape's warm burning blood
(Remember the First Fruit)
knowing ourselves a part of you

FROM "THE PARTAKING" BY LUCI SHAW

This is one of my favorite pictures of my son Ben. Here he's drinking his first bottle of pop. At three years old, he'd had soda before, but always out of a cup. So on this steamy summer day in

1977, his mother and I seated him in a lawn chair and handed him a partially drained bottle of Pepsi. I grabbed my camera and began shooting as he thought about the best way to drink it.

What the photo lacks in composition it makes up in showing how much Ben wanted to get at that sweet nectar in the bottom third of the bottle. It also shows how he couldn't

quite figure out how to do it, having never drunk from a pop bottle before. Finally, he gave up figuring and just shoved the neck of the bottle into his little mouth and tipped the whole thing back. This picture is of him trying to puzzle it out, right before he tipped it back and got doused. His eyes are big, the bottle's neck is stuck deep in his mouth, and an expression of wonder plays on his little round face. After the tipping, he was a sugary, sweet mess as the contents had spilled all over him. That didn't make for nearly as fine a photo.

This picture sums up for me some of the defining aspects of taste, including unbridled thirst, anticipation, savoring and hope. When I look at that picture, Psalm 42:2 comes to mind: "My soul thirsts for God, for the living God" (NIV). Few of us think about seeking God with that kind of thirst or about taste as a way to experience God. Yet Christianity is a faith of tastes. From the informal flavors of coffee and donuts at countless church fellowship hours to the holy taste of the consecrated bread and wine at communion, our faith is formed in no small part by our tongues. "Take, eat: This is my Body, which is given for you," is fraught with spiritual and physical invitation. Yet we often miss the physical connection in our thinking or talking about God. As Mary Gordon reminds us, "The incarnate God is a potent embodiment of what I think of as the truth about the human lot: that we are mixed, flesh, blood, spirit, mind—and that the holy is inseparable, not only from matter, but from the narrative of our lives."

And so, even though the bread and wine possess tastes, we often move through the "tasting" (and other sensory experiences) in rote ways and thereby miss God's teaching us through our bodies.

TASTING THE STORY

Perhaps we should learn from the Jews, our spiritual ancestors. When they celebrate Passover, they intentionally combine words of faith and tastes of faith. The tastes reinforce the story of faith by specifically recalling (in the same way the bread and wine recall Christ's sacrifice) important details of faith.

The foods include

- matzo, placed within the folds of a napkin to represent the haste with which the Israelites fled Egypt
- *maror* (bitter herbs), often horseradish, to symbolize the bitterness of slavery
- *charoset,* a tasty mixture of apples, nuts, wine and cinnamon that recalls the mortar the Jews used as slaves when they were forced to erect Egyptian buildings
- roasted egg *(beitzah)* to symbolize life
- parsley or celery *(karpas),* representing redemption and hope
- the roasted shank bone *(zeroa)* of a lamb that stands for the paschal lamb sacrificed on the first Passover

Additionally, there are four glasses of wine that represent redemption, and a special glass is left for Elijah the prophet, whose presence is anticipated (much in the same way the presence of Christ is anticipated in the consecrated bread and wine).

Even though I am not Jewish, I have had the privilege of participating in Seder meals, thanks to my close friend Aaron and his family. A rabbi, Aaron has often hosted us at Passover. He also invites us to be full participants (at more than one Passover I have read the part of the foolish son—which some thought was typecasting). To this day, when I taste horseradish (which I strangely like) I remember the bitterness of the Jewish enslavement. Tasting the exodus has enhanced my understanding of the exodus.

THE SACRAMENT OF TASTE
One reason that God gave us the sense of taste, besides the sheer enjoyment it gives us, is to bring us closer to the One who loves us

more than we can know. Taste is a tool of faith—a sacrament, if you will. I think taste, as well as the rest of the senses, fits the definition of a sacrament as anything that serves as a visible means of divine grace. My favorite definition comes from Leland Ryken of Wheaton College: "A means of grace, as I use the phrase, is anything in our lives by which God makes his truth and beauty known to us, and correspondingly anything in our lives by which God's presence becomes a reality to us."

Taste is a way that God's presence becomes a reality to us. Not just in bread and wine, but also in the coffee and donuts or meatloaf served at church functions. The divine presence infuses all the tastes around us when God's people gather. Of course, sacramental tastes vary depending upon the rituals of our faith community. For Quakers, who don't observe outward sacraments, it's hard to imagine the taste of bread and wine as a way to experience God's grace. In the same way, it may be difficult for those from a high-church tradition to consider anything less than the consecrated host as a means of grace. Sadly, no matter what our tradition, we place too many limits on the way God teaches us, including using our taste buds.

TASTING GOD DAILY

Have you ever thought about tasting God in what you put in your mouth? The idea that food can remind us of the different attributes, ways and stories of God is a novel thought for most of us.

If I am open to letting God teach me the ways of faith through my body, though, then I can learn the ways of faith through my taste buds as well as my brain. The sweetness of a freshly baked cinnamon roll can remind me of the sweetness of God's love in the same way that horseradish reminds me of the bitterness of slavery. Tasting is a yummy way of spiritual learning!

Recognizing that the tastes we experience daily are carriers of God's wisdom and care for us is possible only if we open ourselves to the possibility that God is truly with us in the everyday. That is how taste teaches us, whether we're gathered at the altar with the people of faith or sitting around our kitchen table with family or swigging on a bottle of pop.

But beware. Just like young Ben with his bottle of pop, we might find ourselves doused in spiritual sweetness and stickiness!

THE TASTE OF FAITH: A SPIRITUAL EXERCISE

In the same way that the Jews use the tastes of various foods to tell their story of faith, I invite you to prepare a menu of faith foods. Pick either a particular faith experience (like the Jews did with Passover) or your entire spiritual journey. Take a few minutes to think about which of those two choices appeals to you more right now.

Once you've chosen, then begin to list tastes that fit your story. What foods mark your journey of faith, either literally or figuratively? Don't think only of good or pleasant tastes; remember how Jews use bitter herbs to remind them of the bitterness of slavery in Egypt. After you come up with the foods or tastes, then create a menu that puts them in an order to illustrate your story.

Once you have your menu together, prepare a meal with these foods. Actually, assemble them to enjoy. As you eat, reflect on your food story with your taste buds, soul and mind. If you don't have the time, or inclination, then have your meal figuratively. Use your imagination to set a table and bring the foods to it. Close your eyes and behold your table spread with your food story of faith. Take time to savor each taste and think of the lessons your story shows you in your soul's imagination.

Sweet, bitter, salty, tangy, rich, bland—the lessons of faith come not just by the words of our mouths, but also by our very mouths themselves. Perhaps that's why the psalmist invites us to "taste and see that the LORD is good!"

2

TASTING FORGIVENESS

by Beth

But you were cleansed; you were made holy;
you were made right with God
by calling on the name of the Lord Jesus Christ.

1 CORINTHIANS 6:11

CLEANSING THE PALATE

David and I had just finished our salads, a variegated assortment
of greens spritzed with a light, tangy dressing, when the waiter
returned to our table with two small plates garnished with a dol-
lop of what looked like Cheese Whiz. It wasn't hard for him to
read the expressions on our youthful faces. At the inexperienced
age of twenty-three, we had no idea what this food was, and so he
said, in a low voice, "To cleanse your palate."

"Ahhhh," we replied, nodding our heads as if the light of dawn
had just illumined our untraveled lives.

We looked at one another, took a spoonful and discovered, to
our surprise, the cool, tingling refreshment of orange sherbet on
our tongues. It all made sense now. This cleansing step, custom-
ary in an upscale restaurant that served delicate seafood, was to
enhance our dining experience. By erasing any lingering flavors of
our salads, we were able to better taste the subtleties of our next
course. Brilliant! (And besides, dessert works for me just about
any time.)

Each morning, I have a similar experience when I reflexively run my tongue over my teeth and notice the invigorating flavor of toothpaste. I have once again succeeded in brushing away morning breath. The crisp, minty taste is a welcomed sensation after the earthy bitterness of coffee has turned stale in my mouth. It's like starting over again, erasing all the evidence of the past, the residue of undesirable flavors; it's the opportunity to "cleanse the palate" in order to savor what is to come. I imagine my taste buds standing at attention, ready for their next assignment.

Stop and notice the taste in your mouth. Is it a good or bad taste? Do you notice residual flavors left over from your most recent meal? Do you wish you could cleanse your palate right now?

One of the ways our senses awaken us to God is through prompting us to connect our physical condition with our spiritual condition. Just as garlicky salad dressing and strong coffee leave a residual taste in our mouths that beg for cleansing, so do actions and attitudes that head us down a path *away* from God. Those movements and their consequences often leave an indelible but sometimes barely perceptible "bad" taste in our spirits. The biblical term used to describe stances that are off-center from God's desires for us is *sin*. Sin tarnishes our lives and requires cleansing much like our palate, in order for us to become receptive to the tastes of a new day and to fresh promptings of the Spirit.

Have you experienced a time when you felt the residue of sin? I remember a time when I could do little *but* notice its filmy deposit. I was a freshman in college, and though it was springtime, I felt weighed down in an oppressive fog of guilt. One day as I walked to class, my backpack slung over my shoulder, I read a little booklet called *Jesus Pocket Promises* (it *was* the '70s). This book was a compilation of Bible verses listed topically. I had turned to the subject of forgiveness.

I did so because I felt stained from sin. I needed to be forgiven and I knew it. However, I had made so many bad choices, I wasn't sure God could ever forgive me. As I walked along, I read Isaiah 1:18, "Though your sins are like scarlet, I will make them as white as snow. Though they are red like crimson, I will make them as white as wool." The imagery was so vivid—the stark contrast between blood-red scarlet and pure white snow, between brilliant red crimson and downy white wool. I read the verses and queried, "Could it be that God has the capacity to forgive me?" What felt like a fresh, cool breeze washed over me and caused a draft of hope to enter my heart.

Do you remember a time when you longed for release from guilt and shame? You craved the sensation of being clean again, of having the weight of your offenses carried from you and the lightness of forgiveness restored? Have you ever resisted forgiving someone and felt oppressed by your anger and the venom of unforgiveness? How can something so integral to our faith, a core teaching of Christianity, the central heart of the gospel of grace, be so profoundly difficult to experience as reality? Why can't we taste a cleansing of the palate of our hearts?

WHY WE DON'T TASTE FORGIVENESS

Forgiveness is an ethereal concept offered to us by an invisible God. (If only God came as a waiter to our table with orange sherbet!) When Jesus spent his last moments with his disciples before his arrest, he did so at a meal. He chose the elements of wine and bread to embody his sacrifice for the forgiveness of sins. Jesus invited them to receive the cup and the morsel, take them into themselves, and taste forgiveness. He anticipated and commemorated his death on the cross for the forgiveness of sins through the sense of taste. *Perhaps we don't experience the cleansing power of forgiveness because we have quit tasting it.*

Sure, many of us participate in receiving communion weekly or monthly—some even daily. Yet we can go through the motions without really tasting the divine meal. In many traditions, communion has been stripped of its sensory impact. We rush through the experience to get to the "real meal"—the sermon. Jesus purposefully used the tangible stuff of bread and wine to help his disciples hear, see, feel, smell and taste forgiveness—to bring forgiveness into them as they ingested it. It's important for us to do the same today.

While the concept of being forgiven (to cancel a debt, to send away) is easy to grasp intellectually, the challenge comes when we try to grasp it experientially—so that it's a lived reality. How do we come to know deep within our hearts that we are fully forgiven by God? How do we forgive ourselves? And perhaps hardest yet, how do we forgive those who have hurt us deeply? It is a process, for sure. To give the impression that it is done in one single act is misleading. But while we have to be actively involved in the process, we can't receive forgiveness or offer forgiveness without God's enabling.

Through this kinesthetic experience, you will be invited to taste God's forgiveness more fully and then offer forgiveness to anyone toward whom you might be harboring bitterness. (You will need your journal, a cup with a few teaspoons of vinegar in it and a peppermint for this exercise.)

TASTING FORGIVENESS AND UNFORGIVENESS: A SPIRITUAL EXERCISE

Tasting unforgiveness. In your cup is vinegar. In a moment, you will taste it, a little bit at a time. It represents the bitterness of unforgiveness—something Scripture describes that happens when we fail to receive forgiveness or refuse to forgive. "Look after each other so that none of you fails to receive the grace of God. Watch out that no poisonous root of bitterness grows up to trouble you, corrupting many" (Hebrews 12:15).

• Take a comfortable posture and breathe three deep breaths

slowly. Hallow this moment, bring full attention to it, and invite God to be with you.

- Take a sip of the vinegar. Let it saturate your mouth, cheeks, tongue, the roof of your mouth and your taste buds.

- Ask the Spirit to show you where there is bitterness in your heart *toward yourself*—something for which you haven't forgiven yourself. Pay attention to what comes to mind. Don't shame yourself. God isn't accusing you or condemning you. He wants to forgive and heal you.

- Take another sip. Taste it. Let the bitterness soak in. Ask the Spirit to lead you through the taste to any bitter root in your heart *toward someone else*. Again, just listen, but don't shame yourself. God wants to free you to forgive.

- Take another sip and then ask God to show you if you have any bitterness *toward him*—for some way that he has disappointed you or let you down.

- Take a few moments and write down any bitter taste of unforgiveness that you identified.

Tasting forgiveness. What does forgiveness taste like? Take your peppermint, open it, smell it and hold it in the palm of your hand. This peppermint represents the cleansing of sin described in 1 John 1:9, "But if we confess our sins to him, [God] is faithful and just to forgive us our sins and to cleanse us from all wickedness."

- Resume a comfortable posture of prayer, put the peppermint in your mouth, and allow the flavor to permeate and cleanse your palate. As you suck on the mint, allow it to wash away all the bitter taste of the vinegar.

- If the Spirit brought to mind any bitterness in your heart toward yourself, name that right now. Taste the cleansing mint in your mouth and imagine God's forgiveness washing over that issue. Receive forgiveness for it and for all your sins through the death of Christ. 1 Corinthians 6:11 says, "But you were cleansed; you were made holy; you were made right with God by calling on the name of the Lord Jesus Christ and by the Spirit of our God." Confess to yourself: "I am cleansed. I am holy. I am right with God." Thank him.

- If the Spirit brought to mind any bitterness in your heart toward another, name that person and picture his or her face. As you taste the peppermint, imagine forgiveness washing over the wound caused by this person. Let it be a healing balm in this wound. Now offer this person forgiveness from the supply of forgiveness in your own heart. Scoop some up and present it to the person as a gift. Matthew 6:14 says, "If you forgive those who sin against you, your heavenly Father will forgive you." Confess to God that you forgive him or her.

- Finally, if the Spirit brought to mind any bitterness toward God, name what that is to God. Tell him why you hurt. Ask God to remove any blockage between you; ask him to heal your heart and restore intimacy with him. Read these words of Asaph in Psalm 73:21-23, 25:

> Then I realized that my heart was bitter,
>   and I was all torn up inside.
> I was so foolish and ignorant—
>   I must have seemed like a senseless animal to you.
> Yet I still belong to you;
>   you hold my right hand. . . .
> Whom have I in heaven but you?
>   I desire you more than anything on earth.

- Take a moment and acknowledge your desire for God. Record anything that is important for you to express.

We know that it isn't through a peppermint that we have been forgiven, but through the blood of Christ, the son of God. Through his forgiveness, he has washed away all that has turned rancid in our hearts. Savor his forgiveness like the welcomed sensation of brushed teeth after the bitterness of coffee has turned stale in your mouth. Start over today, your spiritual taste buds standing at attention, receptive to the tastes of a new day and to fresh promptings of the Spirit.

3

KEEPING KOSHER

by Brent

Please
If it's not too late
Make it a cheeseburger.

LYLE LOVETT

I ate a hamburger. And not just any hamburger—this was a big ol' half-pound bacon-and-sharp-cheddar-cheese hamburger, with a side of fries loaded with salt. Talk about what the doctor didn't order! So to make it healthier, I loaded it with lettuce, onions, pickles and tomatoes. I washed it all down with a diet root beer.

Yeah, as if the diet soda and the vegetable toppings canceled out the grease and sodium and fat and excess carbs.

Still, it was yummy. I'd forgotten how good a "real" hamburger tastes as compared to some slapped-together thing from a fast-food place. I savored it. I didn't feel guilty . . . at the time. Though I should have, breaking kosher as I was.

Now, unlike my rabbi friend Aaron, I don't keep "true" kosher. Not as Jews understand kosher. I keep what I call "diabetic kosher"—a list of foods that are okay for me to partake of and a list of foods that ain't.

Cheeseburgers and fries are on the "ain't" list.

The great reformer Martin Luther said that if we were going to sin, that we should do so boldly. I took his advice, dietetically speaking, to taste buds.

FOOD AS BLESSING

My breaking diabetic kosher with the cheeseburger (a diabetic sin!) was the cause for some reflection (sinning, major or minor, often does that to me). The idea of kosher comes from Leviticus and all the dietary laws listed there about the foods that are okay to eat and those that aren't. There are also laws about how food is to be prepared and served. It all seemed rather complicated to me, so I asked Aaron about it. He gave me a long discourse on keeping kosher, which he summarized by saying that the point of kosher is to make sure you eat food that blesses your body and to remember and give appreciation to the source of that food— God. My diabetic kosher diet plan blesses my body—though I had never thought of it that way before—by ensuring (so long as I follow it) that I eat the right combinations of foods to keep my diabetes in control.

The idea of eating that which blesses our bodies helps us look in fresh ways at the tastes that pass over our palates. What do you understand "blessing" to mean? The blessing may be one of pure enjoyment. And that's a fine blessing in itself, a true gift from God. But as you think about taste in this new way, you might discover some blessings you hadn't thought of before in what you're eating. Take a minute and think of the foods that make your mouth water, that really get your taste buds standing at attention. Then go a bit deeper and ask:

- What foods bless me?

- Why do I think of these tastes or foods as a blessing?

- How do they bless me?

- Do they help me remember that they were a gift from God?

As you think about the things that feed your body and tickle your taste buds, let them help you consider the things that feed your spirit. Have you ever thought of them as a blessing? Think about things that bless your soul. Now ask those same questions, albeit with a slight twist:

- What blesses my spirit?

- Why do I think of these things as blessings?

- How do they bless me?

- Do I see my blessings as coming from God's bounty?

EATING THE HOURS

Another part of keeping diabetic kosher is keeping time. Instead of eating two or three times a day, I eat all day. Well, that's how it seemed at first. The idea is to put food into my body at the times it needs it to run smoothly and keep the sugars in balance. In that way, it is sort of a physical version of the spiritual practice of praying the hours, the formal praying at specific times throughout the day that many Christians use to feed their souls. In the Psalms we read, "Evening, morning and noon I cry out in distress, and he hears my voice" (Psalm 55:17 NIV). This centuries-old practice of praying the hours was Christianized when the early apostles and other Christians followed their Jewish roots and prayed at specific times of the day and night. Eventually, many Christians (Catholic, Orthodox, Anglican and others) began observing this practice in the following form:

Lauds or Dawn Prayer
Prime or Early Morning Prayer
Terce or Mid-morning Prayer
Sext or Midday Prayer
None or Mid-afternoon Prayer
Vespers or Evening Prayer
Compline or Night Prayer (before heading to bed)

In the same way they use prayer, I use food to feed my physical body. I eat the hours:

7:00 a.m.	Oatmeal and coffee
10:00 a.m.	Healthy snack of a granola bar and light yogurt
Noon	Well-balanced lunch
3:00 p.m.	Healthy snack of some pretzels and a box of raisins or a banana
6:00 p.m.	Well-balanced supper
9:00 p.m.	A glass of milk and three ginger snaps

Eating the hours did not come naturally to a free-spirited body and soul. I am not used to liturgy, either spiritual or physical. So my first steps consisted of learning this regimented behavior. In the early days, I had to force myself to follow it. Now it is a part of my life. It comes naturally. Eating the hours keeps me in balance, which is something I need both physically and spiritually.

A FLAVORFUL LITURGY: A SPIRITUAL EXERCISE

My practice of eating the hours also helps me think about my spiritual exercises and ways of incorporating them into my daily life. It reminds me that even if I start my day with a well-balanced meal of Bible reading and prayer, that is not the only spiritual meal I need to partake of during the day. I find that I must feed myself spiritually around the clock, in the same way I feed my body. My spiritual feeding schedule needs to include

- breaks for spiritual silence so I can listen to and for God's voice
- time to read a wee book of poems as prayers
- music
- art
- more spiritual silence

As you think about your ideal eating times, ask yourself how, or if, they line up with your spiritual needs. Are there certain times in the day that you can feel yourself needing a shot of spiritual power? What sort of spiritual food or snack do you need then?

Write a spiritual menu for your day. Pick the times you need nourishment and fill your menu with the things that feed your soul. Are there spiritual practices that you could tie in with your mealtimes? Recall the list that you thought up earlier of things that feed your spirit and bless your soul, and then consider whether one or more of them might fit at

- breakfast
- mid-morning coffee break
- lunch
- mid-afternoon snack
- supper
- bedtime snack

"Food, glorious food," the workhouse boys from the musical *Oliver!* sing. Food, and its glorious tastes, brings us closer to the God who sustains and feeds us all. Taste blesses us.

4

CRAVINGS

by Beth

Like newborn babies, you must crave pure spiritual milk
so that you will grow into a full experience of salvation.
Cry out for this nourishment, now that you have
had a taste of the Lord's kindness.

1 PETER 2:2-3

Within minutes of finishing dinner, I often become aware of an unsolicited craving for a piece of dark chocolate. Like one of Pavlov's dogs, at the sound of the bell—usually clanging dishes in the sink—I subconsciously begin to think about, even fixate on, chocolate. Convinced that my meal is not complete without this bittersweet finale, I head to the upper cabinet to the left of my stove, where I keep my "stash." If you went there now, you would find a stack of Trader Joe's dark chocolate bars, the top one opened, the wrapper folded partway back. Like a ritual, I break off three small squares in a row and take what David and I affectionately call our "vitamin." ("Do you want your vitamin?" we say to one another.) I take small bites and relish each in order to extend the duration of this sublime experience. Then, for several minutes, I savor the rich, smooth, full-bodied flavor of dark chocolate as it lingers in my mouth. (By chance, do you find yourself craving dark chocolate about now?)

From where does this craving come? What compels me to think, desire and act upon it? I'm sure it's partially conditioning. I've trained myself to crave dark chocolate at the end of a meal because I have eaten dark chocolate habitually after meals for some time now. My mind, body and soul associate chocolate with pleasure. I don't have to talk myself into satisfying my longing; I do it without thinking.

I suspect that my craving also comes from a fondness for this particular brand of sweets. I have a penchant for *dark* chocolate. As a little girl, I remember my grandmother preferring dark chocolate over milk chocolate. When she had a box of Russell Stover Candies, which was almost always, all the dark candies would disappear, and the light ones were left for me. Nowadays, like my grandmother, I typically prefer a little bitterness with the cocoa flavor. It stays with me longer and is more satisfying.

I also know that cravings come from physiological needs within my body. Now, I am not justifying my chocolate fetish as if it satisfies some innate physical need, a vitamin or mineral of which my body is deficient. I wish! But when I was pregnant, for instance, I craved foods that were rich in iron—something my body needed to sustain its health and the health of my baby. Eggs and spinach, as an example, were foods that sounded good to me.

Cravings are a curious thing.

- They come out of nowhere.

- They are individual and instinctive.

- They are unquestionably persistent and persuasive. (They've been known to be so strong that they send people out in the middle of the night for a quart of Häagen-Dazs.)

- And they often won't go away until they are fed.

Take a moment right now and think about the foods you crave. What are they? Are they salty or sweet? Spicy or savory? Creamy or crunchy? When do you notice them—at the same time every day, or when you are bored, anxious or ready to relax?

CRAVING PURE SPIRITUAL MILK

Just as we experience strong, physical cravings for certain foods, we also have spiritual cravings that compel us to taste the goodness of God. Peter encouraged the believers in Rome, "Like newborn babies, you must crave pure spiritual milk so that you will grow into a full experience of salvation. Cry out for this nourishment, now that you have had a taste of the Lord's kindness" (1 Peter 2:2-3). He saw a correlation between what we crave (pure spiritual milk) and how we grow (into a full experience of salvation). Peter used the analogy of a newborn who urgently roots for his or her mother's breast, having tasted the wonderful sustenance of her milk and wanting more. The mother's milk maintains the life of this little one who is incapable of consuming or digesting any other form of nourishment. The mother's milk satisfies this baby's hunger—not only through its nutrients but also through the closeness of nursing. This is an image that Peter used to speak to us about spiritual cravings.

Peter described the food we are to crave as pure spiritual milk. "Pure" conveys the idea that it is wholesome and uncontaminated. Spiritual milk comes from the Spirit and nourishes us just as food feeds the body. If you've ever been with nursing infants, you know what it's like when they are hungry. Peter said that once we have "tasted" the kindness of the Lord (God's mercy and grace), we will be just like them.

DEVELOPING SPIRITUAL CRAVINGS

We can increase our spiritual hunger for God in ways similar to how we develop a craving for certain foods. By *conditioning* ourselves to crave, noticing our *inherent* cravings, and discovering *new and different* cravings, we can enlarge our passion for God and the life that he longs for us to live.

Condition your craving. Just as I have made a habit of turning to the cupboard to the left of my stove for my chocolate fix, so we can condition ourselves to habitually turn to God and cultivate a craving for God. Establishing regular rhythms of spiritual practices is the key. For a very long time, my normal morning cadence has been to draw near to God through prayer, reading Scripture, journaling and meditating. I would undoubtedly suffer spiritual lethargy without consistently positioning myself to experience the presence of God. Daily rhythms are like being the captain of a ship and aligning ourselves with the North Star—they keep us on course and reaffirm the direction of our lives. We won't necessarily follow the same practice every day nor have an epiphany with each endeavor, but cultivating a regular regimen draws us into the presence of Christ. We will begin to crave time with him.

Notice your inherent cravings. Conditioning is important. However, just as each of us has unique food preferences—salty, sweet, spicy or crunchy—we each have a proclivity toward certain paths that most naturally connect us with God. Gary Thomas, in *Sacred Pathways,* describes several means through which we organically bond with God. Things like nature, study, friendship, service, beauty, contemplation and activism are among the list of preferred means of spiritual connection. For me, I know that nature, study and contemplation are primal instincts as I seek to know and live in Christ. I will probably never cease practicing these disciplines. They are mainstays of my spiritual regimen. In the same way, you will have an affinity for particular trails that most naturally lead you toward God. Noticing them will aid you in nurturing your appetite for God.

Discover new and different cravings. Along with conditioning ourselves to crave God and noticing our unique pathway toward God, at different times in our lives we need *different* experiences and *new* practices to gather us into the presence of God and nurture the life of Jesus within. I often talk with people who confess to feeling like they're in a spiritual wasteland. As we explore their life rhythms, it's obvious that they have gotten into a rut. For whatever reason, many of them feel as though there is a "right way" to pursue God. They don't feel the freedom to ask, "What do I want?"—like when craving something and opening the refrigerator to see what sounds good. I encourage people to take a break from the way they typically approach their spiritual rhythms and ask the question, "What does my soul long for?" "What do I need right now?" Often it's something new or different that adds variety and breadth to our encounter with God. You might find exercises in this book helpful for those moments when you find yourself in a dry spell or rut.

I don't know your peculiar food cravings—black olives, green onions, chips and salsa, or pickled pig's feet (that was what my mom craved when she was pregnant—no kidding!). Cravings *are* a curious thing. It's hard to determine their origin. Yet it's clear they have convincing power and an unrelenting commitment to be satisfied. In the following exercise, take some time to learn about your physical and spiritual cravings and tap into the energy they provide to refresh your life.

INDULGE YOUR CRAVINGS: A SPIRITUAL EXERCISE

In this activity, you will need to have on hand a food that you crave and your journal. Please record your thoughts in your journal in the most natural and least cumbersome way. Use bullet points, write in prose, draw pictures and symbols, or do a mind map. The important thing is that you don't become frustrated with journaling—many find it hard—and unable to express your inner thoughts.

- Write down the name of the food that you have selected. Take a bite or drink and describe the flavor, texture and what you like about the taste.

- Take another bite or drink. Think about when you crave this food. List the times of day and/or your emotional state of being when you crave this food most.

- Reflect on how you were introduced to this taste. When did you first begin craving it? How have you conditioned yourself to continue craving it?

- What does your craving for the taste of this food reflect about you—your personality, your preferences, your penchants?

- Now think of craving as a spiritual metaphor. If you could name what you crave right now in your relationship with God, what would it be?

- What sounds good to you? What experience would satisfy your craving? Journal your responses.

- Take another bite or drink of your favorite food. Is there a similarity or connection between your food craving and your spiritual craving? Journal your responses.

5

SPIRITUAL SMORGASBORD

by Brent

And he became very hungry, and would have eaten:
but while they made ready, he fell into a trance, And saw heaven
opened, and a certain vessel descending upon him, as it had been a great
sheet knit at the four corners, and let down to the earth: Wherein were
all manner of fourfooted beasts of the earth, and wild beasts,
and creeping things, and fowls of the air. And there came
a voice to him, Rise, Peter; kill, and eat.

ACTS 10:10-13 (KJV)

Besides being fun to say, *smorgasbord* is the word that best describes the usual tastes of my life. Except for breakfast. Breakfast tastes consist of coffee and oatmeal.

But unlike the sameness of my breakfast flavors, most of the tastes of my life, probably like yours, are smorgasbordish. During one four-day period when Beth and I were doing Thirty Days of Tasting, I noticed a wide range of flavors cross my palate, one of them being "almost duck." "Almost duck" is when your friendly neighborhood chef comes out from the back to visit with you and you ask, "So, got any duck on the menu tonight?" and he says, "Not really, but I'll fix duck for you" and you say, "Cool"; and then when the duck gumbo comes and you dig in, you realize, after a few bites, that there is a distinctive flavor you haven't experienced for a while; you look down and see "SHRIMP!!!!!" in the dish; you're allergic to shellfish, and your friendly neighborhood chef forgot that you were allergic to shellfish and so put shrimp in for you, just to make it special, and you then cannot eat the meal you're hungry for. Your friendly neighborhood chef is feeling horrible because he almost poisoned you, and you're feeling bad because it wasn't his fault and you don't want him to feel bad, and you end up having chicken gumbo, which is very good and which you call "almost duck" from that night on.

While "almost duck" was the most memorable gustatory sensation of those four days, I also experienced flavors ranging from chicken chili to cheese and crackers to thick French toast and fried eggs to beer to lamb chops to smoked salmon to bottled water to wine to goldfish (the cracker kind) to . . . well, you get the idea. Your culinary life has probably been much the same. What are some of the tastes that have traveled across your tongue the past few days? Make a quick list of them now. What flavors can you recall?

A TASTE OF BLESSING

As you thought of the many tastes that have passed over your palate, did you think about deeper things you might learn from them? I often don't. When I am paying attention in love to daily life, though, I find that each taste has some blessing associated with it. That's because the good tastes come from the hand of God.

The idea that all good things in our lives come from God is deeply rooted in Scripture. And that includes food! As the psalmist says,

> Let them give thanks to the LORD for his unfailing love
>   and his wonderful deeds for mankind,
> for he satisfies the thirsty
>   and fills the hungry with good things. (Psalm 107:8-9 NIV)

While it is hardly breaking news that God loves us, we often don't think about food and drink being expressions of that love.

When you look at the tastes of your past few days, did you see God's love in them? I often find God's love reflected in the variety of tastes and textures on my tongue, as well as the blessings of dear friends and engaging conversations. The tastes invoke a sort of communion, where I break bread with people important to me, and we speak of matters important to us, including faith.

As you think of the tastes that you've experienced the past few days, what blessings and lessons do they bring to mind?

The flavors I experienced as blessings became blessings as they were shaped by the actual tastes and the associations that I attach to those tastes—the people, places and conversations that occurred when I was enjoying them—along with the lessons that I learned from them. It is important for me to recognize that the smorgasbord of tastes that comes my way daily is a blessing. Those tastes are gifts from God out of the riches of a bounty prepared for me.

When I pay attention in love to the tastes in my life, I taste

God's goodness to me. That is a lesson I need to keep in mind, especially on days when the buffet is not quite up to my selfish expectations.

THE LESSONS OF TASTE

Scripture is full of a smorgasbord of tastes that do more than merely bless—they teach. Think of the manna God provided for the Israelites on the exodus. Manna was food that was more than food. Each bite reminded the Hebrews on that journey that God sustained them—down to providing daily sustenance. No manna could be stored; God sent it daily. Through it, the Israelites learned that it was God who provided for them—not their own prowess as anglers, hunters or farmers.

In addition to manna, other biblical tastes have lessons associated with them, including goat, quail, honey, fish and locust. These foods show that God teaches his people in many ways, including through our taste buds. Like many of the tastes mentioned in the Bible, the tastes I enjoy often have potential for spiritual learning associated with them too.

- The purity of the water I drink reminds me of the purity toward which I strive. I want to be pure in heart so that I will see God (Matthew 5:8).

- My glasses of grape (no, not Welch's—a Shiraz-Cabernet blend) call to mind Jesus' first miracle of turning water into wine. The wedding host pronounced it "the best" (John 2:10). I need to look for the best—the touch of Jesus—in all that I encounter. This is not always my inclination.

- The first spoonful of oatmeal tastes not only of the creamy richness of milk-covered oats but also serves as a flavorful reminder of my faith tradition. I think about how the Quakers intimately interweave our understanding of the gospel of Jesus Christ into our beliefs in the equality of all people, living simply and peacefully, and experiencing the immediate presence of God in the midst of daily life. With each bite, I resolve to live more closely and fully into those beliefs.

Manna was faith food that the entire community ate. In that way it's similar to how many Christians experience the bread and wine of communion. Bread and wine are faith foods that sustain countless Christ-followers on their conjoined pilgrimage to God. But bread and wine are not the only faith foods God provides.

TASTING DEEPER: A SPIRITUAL EXERCISE

Take a few minutes and think of Bible stories you know that mention food. Or, if you like playing with a computer, go to a Scripture site such as biblegateway.com and do a word search for some of your favorite foods. (No, I didn't find oatmeal, and you probably won't find T-bone or tofu unless there's some interesting new translation out there.) As you look at the verses that mention various foods, consider these questions:

- What lessons do the foods teach?
- Why are they important enough to be included in the Bible?

As you remember the flavors you've experienced the past few days, consider the following:

- What opportunities for spiritual reflection do they offer you?
- Do any of them remind you of the Bible or other spiritual stories?
- Do any call to mind your particular faith tradition or your Christian life?
- What are the flavors of your faith tradition?
- Where do you experience them in the faith community?
- Where else do you taste them?

These tastes that come to us daily could be as commonplace, but as deep, as the taste of a communion wafer dissolving on your tongue, or they could be something completely out of the ordinary like lutefisk, that wonderfully Scandinavian delicacy served by Lutherans in the upper Midwest at Christmastime and other special occasions (and the taste of which makes me glad I'm not one of them). What is one primary taste that speaks of faith to you and why?

6

TASTING WORDS

by Beth

Words kill, words give life;
they're either poison or fruit—you choose.

PROVERBS 18:21 (*THE MESSAGE*)

TASTING VINEGAR

I grew up in a generation of kids who learned a lesson or two from the unpleasant taste of soap. If a child sassed her mom or said a naughty word or mean things to his sibling, the parent would follow protocol and say, "Do you want me to wash your mouth out with soap?" I don't remember my parents ever acting on the threat, but I definitely remember hearing it.

Now, of course, when *my* kids were little, we used a much more civilized method of discipline. Instead of vile-tasting soap, we made them taste a teaspoon of vinegar if they said something unkind to their brother or sister or had a "potty mouth." When they tasted the bitterness, we wanted them to

connect the sour flavor with their spiteful jab or crude language. At the time, it seemed to be an improvement over washing their mouths out with soap. Now that our kids are grown,
however, they love giving us grief about it. Just one more reason why they will all need counseling!

Have you ever connected your sense of taste with the taste of
words? It's hard to believe, but some people actually have a condition called lexical-gustatory synesthesia. (Now that's a mouthful!)
They hear a word and instantly experience a taste in their mouths.
A person might hear words like *fire, smoke* or *arson* and begin to
taste an acrid, scorched flavor. I once had a coworker who hated
the word *moist*. She would get a sickening taste in her mouth if she
heard someone say it. (Of course, we were not terribly sympa-
thetic to her repulsion and would often use the word as many
times as we could in a single sentence.)

Though many of us do not have the condition of lexical-gustatory synesthesia, we do have the ability to distinguish a variety of
flavors from words merely spoken by the tongue. In this case, we
use our sense of taste to "taste" words metaphorically. In fact, because we have the ability to discriminate bitter, salty, sour and
sweet flavors, we also have the facility to savor words and identify
their essence. Think about it: words evoke a variety of "flavors."
Some are sweet and appetizing, while others are bitter and dis-
tasteful. Some bless and build up; others tear down and wound.
Pay attention to your reaction to these words:

- loving

- kind

- good-hearted

- sweet

- honest

- beautiful

- sincere

- valiant

How do these words "taste"?

Now watch your reaction to this list:

- ugly

- ungrateful

- wretched

- cruel

- worthless

- vile

- evil

- despicable

How do you describe their flavors?

As the proverb suggests, "Words kill, words give life; they're either poison or fruit—you choose" (Proverbs 18:21 *The Message*). More than likely, each of us can attest to that fact. We recall instances, even from childhood, when someone spoke specific words that we've never forgotten! They might have been words that made us feel proud and good about ourselves or words that humiliated and hurt us. These words left a taste in our mouths—that of sweet fruit or corrosive poison.

I will never forget the affirming flavor of words my eighth-grade science teacher spoke to me. After a class presentation, he pulled me aside and told me that he saw an aptitude in me that he hadn't noticed before—my gift of public speaking. I'm not sure that I had ever noticed this ability either, but as I *savored* my teacher's comment, I became more curious about it and began to cultivate a gift that was native to me. This is an example of how our literal senses can be applied in a secondary, metaphoric way to understand, take in and experience our lives more deeply. So let's consider what might happen if we use our sense of taste symbolically to taste transforming words.

Whether we realize it or not, we often and involuntarily mull over both loving and unloving words that we have said or others have said to us. Think of what might happen if we intentionally practiced "tasting" life-giving, truth-bearing words. That practice could help us digest and absorb their meaning and significance, transforming mere words into meaningful knowledge. I have found that when I savor affirming words, the harmful ways I think about God, life and myself are disabled. A powerful diet of word-tasting enables us to absorb the nutrients found in God's daily round of vocalized love.

TASTING GOD'S WORD

Scripture uses the sensory metaphor of tasting God's Word as a way to experience its meaning and essence: "How sweet your words taste to me; they are sweeter than honey" (Psalm 119:103). Have you ever "tasted" a word from God? Perhaps you were reading the Bible and certain words in a passage caught your attention. You stopped, read and then reread them, until their meaning became clear and personally significant. This kind of listening to God's Word involves slow, thoughtful exploration—like the way you suck on a butterscotch and extract flavor from it with each roll of your tongue. God speaks to us not only through Scripture but also through a host of mediums: nature, stories, sermons, movies, songs and prayers. Learning to savor words from God initiates a process that enables his Word to nourish our soul.

Perhaps another way to describe this kind of leisurely and deliberate tasting is "contemplation." Contemplation is reflective, thoughtful consideration of something that allows us to know it more intimately and fully. Consider what happens when we contemplate: "Contemplation leads to, or rather is an experience of, transcendence—that is, of forgetfulness of self and of everyone and everything else except the contemplated object." What often distracts us from hearing God's word, echoing through voices all around us, is our inability to be present and to concentrate. We are preoccupied with our own thoughts. We feel sidetracked by what we need to do next. We become unsettled as we notice disturbing feelings that surface once we slow down. However, when we develop the skills of contemplating (tasting) God's Word, we become lost in the beauty and veracity of what he is saying. God's truth looms larger than our own anxiousness and self-absorption.

When I first became acquainted with the Bible, I thought the more I read it, the better. Now I realize that it's more important to make sure I am digesting it. That's where meditating/contemplating/tasting comes in. Learning to deliberate on what I read, sometimes for several days, until I feel I have extracted all that God has in it for me is a valuable practice. This exercise of reflection makes truth more personally profound to me. In turn, God and his love also become more real. I can know in my head that God is *supposed* to love me. But I sometimes don't feel or believe that he *truly* loves me. By slowly tasting his Word, I ingest his love and affection, and it nourishes me.

TASTING ANOTHER'S WORDS

In the same way that we figuratively taste God's Word, we can allow another person's words to penetrate and strengthen our hearts. I'm referring to life-giving words, not ones that are damaging or disparaging. Have you ever been in the midst of a conversation when someone spoke words to you that instantly resonated, as if sounding a bell inside you? Then later, you found yourself remembering and thinking about them? The book of Proverbs describes this experience: "Kind words are like honey—sweet to the soul and healthy for the body" (Proverbs 16:24), and "Wise words satisfy like a good meal; the right words bring satisfaction" (Proverbs 18:20). Your soul tasted words that were sweet and satisfying.

Often resonant words come in the form of a compliment or validation. Someone notices a job well done or recognizes a positive trait in you and affirms it. In that moment, your knowing heart takes hold of the words like a thirsty plant soaking up water. You receive them as nourishment; they are strengthening and confirming. Other times, a person's words express an understanding and knowledge of you. They name something in you with language that has particular meaning, expressing insights in a way that you haven't heard before. When someone speaks words that resonate, we need to taste these words, ponder them and allow their message to sink in. In that way, they instruct, inspire and encourage us.

Once while discussing my vocational calling with my spiritual director, she put a name to what energizes and motivates me. "You are an educator!" she said. For some reason, I had never used that word to describe my passion for teaching and facilitating learning. I wrote it down and kept thinking about it. I realized it named one of my primary motivations, and so I began to use it when I described my vocational desires. Her wise words continue to help me identify opportunities that fit best with the bent of my own soul.

Employing our sense of taste to savor words we hear from God, whatever their source, provides amazing results. Perhaps one of the most gratifying is the transcendent experience of encountering God's presence in the exchange of words. It becomes a sacred moment when you realize that God is the one lifting up the words you are hearing and bringing them to bear upon your life. For example:

- when you read the next lesson in a devotional or chapter in a book and it just happens to converge with a situation in your life for which you need guidance

- when the very passage you turn to in Scripture uses the same language you recently used to describe the condition of your own heart

- when a stranger offers you wise counsel without knowing your life situation
- when suddenly you see something in the natural world that speaks (declares) the glory of God and you are consoled (Psalm 19:1)
- when a friend or spiritual director expresses words that you know come from somewhere other than their own insight

These are the transactions offered each day from a communicative God. For us to receive them, we must slow down enough to taste them. Once we taste them, we must take time to savor them. When we savor them, they become the sweet and satisfying nourishment we need to keep living with courage and strength.

TASTING WORDS: A SPIRITUAL EXERCISE

In the sixteenth century, St. Ignatius of Loyola developed a practice called the Examen of Consciousness or Daily Examen. The purpose of this short period of daily reflection was to seek and find God in all things. Using the basic steps in his model, this exercise will help you think back over the last day or so and identify when you heard words from God or others that quickened your spirit and spoke something important for you to taste and digest.

We sometimes notice words from God and others that have that unique quality of resonance. Yet many times, we let those words roll off us, never giving them the chance to take root. In this exercise, I invite you to think back over your day and isolate any words or expressions, spoken directly or indirectly, that felt powerful to you. Then move through a process of tasting them to help you understand their import and what God might be saying to you through them. I suggest using a journal and pen for this exercise.

- Assume a posture of prayer; acknowledge that you are in God's presence and that he cares for you. Still yourself before him and rest.

- Give thanks to God for being a self-disclosing God who speaks to you each day through Scripture, his word all around you and the words of others.

- Ask the Spirit's help as you review your day. Take time to remember, hour by hour, each interaction you had with God in prayer or with another in conversation. Were any words spoken to you that caught your attention and stirred your heart? Write the words down in your journal as accurately as you can remember them. (It is very possible that you will recall words that were stinging or discouraging. If so, it might be helpful to journal about how they made you feel and why they were hurtful. After you do, ask God to receive these negative words and replace them with his truth. Then imagine God tossing them into a garbage can or out to sea, and return to reviewing your day, recalling life-giving words.)

- Mull over the life-giving words, contemplating or tasting each one. Ask yourself,

  - What do these words taste like?

  - What flavor would I use to describe them?

  - Why do they resonate within me?

  - What do they mean to me?

- Ask God to connect these words with anything that is important for you to recognize. Write down your thoughts.

- Savor these words of life and receive their truth and blessing. Ask God to help you believe them and live them out. Share them with someone you trust.

Part Two

See

Art Reflection on Seeing

As you look at the illustration, take time to relax your body and mind. Breathe deeply. Think about the following questions slowly and gently as you look at this drawing. Savor each thought and each sensory experience that comes to you.

As you contemplate the image of the little girl seated on someone's lap, where is your attention drawn? What would you describe as the focal point of the drawing?

What do you notice about her expression? What does it say to you?

Where do you think she is? Where do you think she is going? Who do you think she is with?

What do you think she is seeing? How does she feel about what she is seeing?

Juliet Benner, in her book Contemplative Vision: A Guide to Christian Art and Prayer, says, "How we see determines what we see, and what we see shapes the soul." Describe how you think this little girl is seeing. How is what she sees shaping her soul?

If you were in this little girl's place, what other senses would be awakened? Describe them.

How are you inspired by this image? How does it make you want to see?

Have you ever found your eyes wide and sparkling with wonder as you caught a glimpse of God?

This piece is titled Wonders Seen (Deuteronomy 10:21). As you think about this piece, what wonders of God that you have seen does it call to mind?

1

INTRODUCTION

by Brent

*The real voyage of discovery consists not in
seeking new landscapes but in having new eyes.*

MARCEL PROUST

I see people. . . . They look like trees walking around." That's from
one of my favorite Bible stories, in Mark 8. Jesus and his disciples
come to the town of Bethsaida, and some friends bring a blind
man to Jesus for healing. Jesus spits (!) on the man's eyes—a very
human act. That shouldn't surprise us. After all, as Sara Miles
says, "Jesus is the Word made flesh. While he lived among us,
what he said and what he did were the same thing. His human
body was God's language, as much as his human speech." So he
spits and then speaks, asking, "Can you see anything now?" The
man answers, "I see people. . . . They look like trees walking
around" (Mark 8:22-24).

I've always wondered how he knew it was people. And why he
thought they looked like trees. How did he know what trees looked
like? I mean, he was blind; what's he know from trees?

Jesus puts his hands on the man's blind eyes a second time, but
there's no spitting in this sequence: "His eyes were opened. His
sight was completely restored, and he could see everything clearly"
(Mark 8:25).

That story makes me wonder. Was it his eyes that were healed
by that second touch—or his perception? Was he given, in addition to an ability to see, the ability to process what he saw and

make sense of it? That wonder came back afresh after reading
Hugues de Montalembert's *Invisible: A Memoir.* In his book, Montalembert tells the story of a man who lost his sight at ten months
and had it restored when he was fifty-three. But the man couldn't
really "see" anything because he wasn't able to make sense of what
his eyes saw. He took in scenes as a camera does. A camera, after
all, does not see; it just records. We need a frame of reference to
make sense of what a camera "sees."

I think the Bethsaida blind man's sight came back because that
second touch by Jesus healed entirely both his body and soul. That
included his ability to perceive, which enabled him to look deeply
into his newly lit world and make sense of it. Perhaps we need
Jesus' touch in that same way.

TAKING A GOOD LOOK

Being able to perceive truly means that we have to pay attention
with our body *and* soul. I know that when I don't, it becomes too
easy to miss the subtle influences of God's Spirit around me. Yes,
my eyes still function—along with my ears, nose, fingers and
mouth. To see God present, however, I must learn to pay attention
with all of me. Too often, I pay attention with part of me while the
rest of me thinks about work that needs doing or any of the myriad other thoughts that crowd my mind. When that happens, as
photographer David Vestal tells us, "You don't have enough attention to see what's around you." If I want to see God present in the
ordinary, in the daily gifts I'm given, I want to move beyond seeing and into perceiving.

Learning to see using our bodies and souls teaches us to receive
the presence of God that surrounds us—in whom we live and
move and have our being. It is not about concocting meaning
where there is none. No. Rather, it is about seeing things aright, as
God intended. Such seeing also centers us in spiritual contemplation. It gets us outside ourselves and reminds us that, no matter

how much we inwardly believe otherwise, it is not all about us. It is about God and the things of God, which includes God's creation. Seeing in this way helps us truly behold the interconnectedness of all of life around us. God ordains and maintains this interconnectedness. In that sense, deep seeing like this is ultimately about revelation.

Seeing with our bodies and souls is a way of actively seeking God. I don't mean just metaphorically with our mind, or spiritually with our soul, but with our physical sight as well. "As creatures who know the world through our senses, the physical world points us to an understanding of the multi-dimensionality of God. We discover the sacred in color, shape, form, scent, touch, and taste," say Christine Valters Paintner and Betsey Beckman.

Discovering the sacred that way is how seeing with our bodies and souls takes us into a fresh and winsome way of living out Jesus' command to "love the Lord your God with all your heart and with all your soul and with all your mind" (Matthew 22:37 NIV).

WHICH IS BETTER—NUMBER ONE OR NUMBER TWO?

Unlike many people, I don't mind going to the eye doctor. In fact, I find it sort of fun. Especially when she pulls the phoropter over (that big old thing with all the dials and lenses and stuff), has me look through it to a chart on the wall, flips lenses back and forth or up and down, and asks, "Which is better? Number one or number two?" It's fun, like a puzzle—a puzzle that puts everything in focus. Literally.

But for the process to work, I have to pay attention. I have to try to see and notice which one does look better. Which one works best makes all the difference for my sight. That's how it is with learning attentiveness to God and God's creation. Seeing in that way is about paying attention to something that is worth paying attention to. Attentive vision opens us to the extraordinary presence of God blessing us in the amazing ordinary. As Madeleine

L'Engle reminds us, "There is nothing so secular that it cannot be sacred, and that is one of the deepest messages of the Incarnation." The best way to learn to see the sacred in the supposed secular is to practice perceiving.

Like any spiritual discipline, learning the art of attentive seeing is not something that happens quickly. Though everything around you can be seen deeply, don't try to behold it all that way at first. Here are some steps you might find helpful:

- Take fifteen minutes and go to a comfortable, familiar place.

- Start with something small. Focus on something manageable—not the entire lifescape around you.

- Now look around the space from as many points of view (or angles) as you can in these few minutes.

- How does shifting your point of view change both what you see and how you see it?

- Is it different when viewed from above than when viewed from below or at eye level?

- Where is the energy in what you're looking at?

- Look at one thing and reflect on what it's showing you about life and God.

- Use your journal to keep notes about what you are seeing.

This exercise may feel unnatural at first. That's because it is. We usually don't slow down and pay attention in love to things around us. But gradually, as we learn to see deeply, we become like the blind man who needed two touches from Jesus—we find our eyes opening and seeing that which may have always been there, but which we finally notice. As documentary photographer Fazal Sheikh says, "The most compelling images have come from remaining receptive to what the place has to offer." I would change that to say that often our most compelling images and experiences of God come from remaining receptive to what the ordinary spaces around us have to offer.

SEEING OUR BEST SELVES

Learning the art of spiritual sight moves us from thinking about faith to experiencing God. It teaches us to sense God at work and play all around us. My faith tradition calls this kind of living "experiential," by which we mean *living* the life of the Spirit and not just *learning* about it. It is the difference between learning about butterflies in a schoolroom and taking a field trip into a meadow to experience them flitting from coneflower to New England aster to black-eyed Susan. Slides and descriptions of butterflies are a good introduction to the concept of butterflies, but experiencing them gives us an entirely different, deeper kind of knowledge.

Ultimately, that's what seeing spiritually is about—deeper knowledge. Yes, it is about seeing God at work around us, but it is also about coming closer to God and to the selves Christ calls us to be. When I take time to see God at work in me, I see the me that God sees. As Meister Eckhart said, "The eye with which I see God is the same as that with which God sees me. My eye and the eye of God are one eye, one vision, one knowledge, and one love. My eye and the eye of God are one."

SEEING SPIRITUALLY: A SPIRITUAL EXERCISE

Spiritually seeing shows us God and our best selves. Remember the exercise on page 62 about mindfulness of ordinary things? Now adapt this exercise to your spiritual life—it's easy to do by shifting the questions slightly.

- Take fifteen minutes and go to a place where you can sit comfortably.

- Start by looking at part of your life that has been on your heart. Focus on something manageable—not your entire interior lifescape.

- Now look at the piece of your heart that captured your attention from as many points of view as you can in these few minutes—from your own perspective, your best friends' and God's.

- How does shifting your point of view change both what you see and how you see it?

- Where is God in what you're looking at?

- What is this showing you about your life with God?

Keep your observations about your spiritual life in the same journal in which you're jotting down your other discoveries. Your journal notes will help you see the amazing interconnectedness of all of your life. They will also spark your wonder and thereby increase your ability to truly see, because "wonder is the fuel which sustains vision."

Your wonder and attentive sight will further awaken you to the wonder of God.

2

CREATURELY INSIGHT

by Beth

Take a lesson from the ants, you lazybones.
Learn from their ways and become wise!

PROVERBS 6:6

It was an early morning in late fall and the last day of my Thirty Days of Seeing experiment. As I opened the back door to let the dog out, I noticed the muted twilight of daybreak. Then something caught my eye. I spotted movement through the trees—the large, broad wings of a bird as it landed on a limb. My first thought was, "It's an owl!" but I questioned my judgment, having never seen an owl in my backyard. I took a good look—a long, steady gaze—and felt hopeful that it was indeed a great horned owl. Quickly and quietly, I closed the door, turned out the lights and searched for a better view. Peering out the kitchen window, I saw it—statuesque on a limb, looking like a huge cat caught in the lofty bough of a tree.

Soon after, David came downstairs, and together we watched through binoculars this wonderful, awesome creature as it preened itself, rotated its head and slept. Most amazingly, it remained on that limb *all* day! I watched it on and off until darkness fell—the last semblance of the owl's presence, the haunting sound of its hooting. It was such a marvelous experience! I found myself overwhelmed with wonder, enamored with the creaturely habits of this unanticipated visitor.

This isn't the first time that I have been amazed and instructed by one of God's brilliant characters from the animal kingdom. Have you ever had an unusual encounter with a creature like this and experienced the wonder of God as you noticed its ways?

For several weeks afterward, I pondered the memory of the owl. Each time its image came to mind, for some reason, it prompted a deep, yearning prayer to God. I was drawn to ruminate on this magnificent creature, and as I did, I began to marvel at its peculiarities. Not unlike the proverb that says, "Take a lesson from the ants, you lazybones. Learn from their ways and become wise!" (Proverbs 6:6), I took lessons from this owl. Through noticing its ways of being and behaving, I gleaned some wonderful insights about life. What would it be like for you to learn from the curious creatures that cross your path?

PAY ATTENTION TO BEING

One of the ways we pay attention to animals is to notice their way of being in the world. What is their posture and presence like? How do they occupy their habitat or relate to other living things around them? At what pace do they move? How do they rest? What do we notice as we study their appearance?

Every time I returned to the window that day to see if my friend was there, I was amazed that it hadn't moved. It never occurred to me that owls, who are nocturnal creatures, likely choose to sleep in one "bed" during the day—though to my knowledge, none had ever chosen a bed in my backyard. As I studied its posture, it appeared to be resting, yet it was an alert rest. Its eyes were sometimes open, sometimes shut. It was *very* still. I sensed no plans to take flight. The owl's demeanor was peaceful as it remained firmly planted on the limb, quietly observing the world beneath it.

As I watched it and later pondered, I thought about how deliberate rest and keen observation go hand in hand. The latter is impossible to achieve without the former. I can't expect to see well unless I become still—deliberately still. When I am rushing about, barely touching down into life, I can't notice the wonder and wisdom of God because it often comes from a deep place that requires listening and observing in order to perceive.

I know that owls are masters at seeing movement in dark, distant places. Their extremely large, forward-facing eyes permit a greater ability for depth perception—especially at night while hunting in the dark. In the same way, insights form in us through the posture of active rest or stillness. It is from this way of being that we discern the flicker of light, the movement of God in the deep waters of our own souls. For us to find our way in this world, we must be willing to perch for suspended periods, simply observing life, looking for unperceived paths that we might otherwise miss.

PAY ATTENTION TO BEHAVIOR

As we observe a creature's way of being in the world, we will naturally notice their unique and often quirky behaviors. Have you ever been amused by the antics of a squirrel scampering in the woods? Or found yourself enthralled with the flight of a swarm of starlings overhead? Is it nearly impossible to drive by a fenced field of horses and not gawk at their spectacular beauty and grace? Whether we observe our own domesticated pets or red foxes in the wild, creatures have a way of enriching our experience of God, of increasing our appreciation of the genius of our Creator, of teaching us through their own life skills.

When I observed the behaviors of the owl, what amused me most was its ability to turn its head practically backwards. In fact, sometimes it was hard to tell if it was looking at me or away from me. I learned that an owl's head can move almost all the way around—270 degrees—because their eyes *can't* move back and forth.

The owl looked circumspectly at its surroundings. What would it mean for me to be circumspect? I thought about looking backwards at my past and what I have learned from it. I thought about looking forward and musing, *Where do I want to go? What direction do I want my life to take?* Then I considered looking at my sides, at the counsel of my friends—those who walk closest with me, know me and care for me. Being circumspect helps fill in the picture of my life and identify the key factors that influence my journey. Being circumspect helps me consider all the angles of my life and discern the best path forward. It allows me to collect insight from the east and west and discernment from the north and south, and then act on it.

Through observing the owl's being and behavior, I took this odd bird into my heart and was ministered to by it. Its visit became a gift from God to me. In the same way, as we attend to the plethora of living creatures that nibble at the edges of our lives, scurry in front of our feet or grace our horizons, we are enlarged by their presence and playfulness, instructed by their manner and habits. Jesus said to us, "Look at the ravens. They don't plant or harvest or store food in barns, for God feeds them. And you are far more valuable to him than any birds!" (Luke 12:24). So, by all means, "Look!" and see what you can learn.

SEEING CREATURELY INSIGHT:
A SPIRITUAL EXERCISE

In this exercise, I invite you to follow the suggestion from the proverb that tells us to "go to the ants" to learn from them. You don't have to choose an ant, but you will have the opportunity to identify a creature to observe, learn about and contemplate. This experience may take a few days or weeks to fulfill. Or, like me, you may have a serendipitous encounter with a creature that will haunt your memory and stay with you for a very long time.

The world is crammed full with astoundingly beautiful creatures, great and small, that have a lot to teach us. Which one do you find most bright and beautiful? A butterfly or a honeybee? A hummingbird or a blue heron? A golden retriever or a calico cat? A chipmunk or a bunny? A dolphin or a sea turtle?

- Have you noticed any interesting creature recently as you were driving along or looking out a window? Have you seen a picture or watched a show where you learned about an animal that intrigues you?

- Ask God to help you notice your "ant"—the creature in your world through which God wants to meet you and speak to you. Over the next day or so, keep your eyes open and see what crosses your path.

- Once you have identified an animal, take time to study it. If you can't observe it in its natural habitat, find a picture or video online and observe it. Do some research and learn about its behaviors and peculiarities.

- As you contemplate this creature, ask God to touch you and teach you through it. Mull over what you discover, and record your thoughts in your journal.

- Draw a picture or include a photograph so that you can remember your icon of creaturely insight.

3

REFRAME AND REFOCUS

by Brent

I am still confident of this:
I will see the goodness of the LORD
in the land of the living.

PSALM 27:13 (NIV 1984)

For once, the weather forecasters were right. The ice storm hit just when they said it would and just as hard. The entire middle part of Indiana was hunkered down, hoping that the ice buildup and high winds would not result in massive power outages and in people finding themselves stranded in their cars out on stretches of rural roads. At the farm, the wood was stacked, food stashed in the fridge and water bottled just in case. For our part, we were lucky. Our power stayed on. And there was no place we had to go. We stayed put and listened to the ice hit and the wind howl.

The next morning I woke to the amazing vista of ice. Everything was covered and glistening—trees, windows, pickup truck,
rocks, fence rails, bird feeders, light fixtures, an old wagon. I beheld a world wrapped in crystalline dazzlement. I knew I'd have to
brave the wind and cold and venture out with my camera. I needed
to capture these scenes that sparkled from what little light poked
through the leaden clouds.

After breakfast, I struggled into my Carhartt coveralls, pulled
on a stocking cap, grabbed my camera and headed out. As I stepped
off the relative warmth of the windowed porch, an amazingly vast
scene overwhelmed me. I began snapping away.

REFRAME

After a few shots, I checked the previews. I was unsatisfied with
the photographs.

This is one of them. You can see why I was dissatisfied. It doesn't
convey what I imagined it would—the power of the ice. The ingredients are all there: ice-covered ground, ice-covered trees, ice-
covered fence rails, ice-covered house. But it's, um, flat. It evokes
no emotion at all.

Then I thought of one of my favorite photographers (and one of the few I know who has a Master of Divinity degree), Freeman Patterson. He says that "letting go of self is an essential precondition to real seeing." So the first thing I had to do was let go of myself and my preconceived ideas about ice storms and how to photograph them, and ask some questions that Patterson says are essential:

- What is the theme or subject?
- What is the subject matter?
- How does the subject matter express the subject?
- What is positive about this new viewpoint?
- What can I learn?

So, taking a step back inside to think (and warm up), I pondered awhile. The subject was the ice storm and how it covered everything. The subject matter was all the stuff covered in ice. To see the stuff covered in ice would show the viewer that the ice falls on everything (the just and the unjust?), coating it with a special, but potentially deadly, glamour.

Armed with those answers, I went back outside and surveyed the scene. My previous photographs had shown me clearly that I could not capture the story of the ice storm with one big picture. Now, this was something I already knew in my photographer's heart, but in my anxiousness to get out and get at it, I "forgot" that I knew it. I needed a bit of a breather to recall Patterson's wisdom. Now I was ready to begin photographing, knowing I would have to reframe the story into a number of smaller vignettes: individual trees, a bent sapling, fence rails.

I went back outside and looked for those little stories. I reframed. I made the scene more manageable. And the photos became more interesting to me and anybody else who might see them. By taking in the essential part of the story, I could then frame it in such a way that it would make sense to the viewer and have power that the photographs of the entire ice-covered farm lacked.

All around you are the big scenes that make up your daily life. How could you reframe the things that you see so they can tell you a new story? Are there certain things that your eyes land upon daily that are so immense that they need to be reframed so you can truly see, and learn from, them afresh? Your scene may be as physically vast as a cityscape or as emotionally huge as a room in a home that is not yours. Regardless, when we try to take in the entire scene set before our eyes, we often find ourselves over-whelmed. The largeness renders us unable to make meaning of it or interpret it for others. It is only as we reframe it that we can capture its essence in a way that makes sense.

Look around now. As you take in all that your sight falls upon, shift your brain to reframing mode and give your eyes permission to rest on whatever grabs their attention. What captures your eyes' and brain's attention? Why do you think what you're seeing calls for attention? Is this a place to begin reframing so that you can let go of yourself and really see?

REFOCUS
While I was still outdoors, I looked at the new, reframed pictures. They were much stronger, like this one—a single tree covered in ice against the cloudy sky.

Still, they lacked a certain depth of feeling I hoped for. Then I thought of something else that Patterson said. He said photogra-phers need to think sideways, which he describes as examin-ing the rules we build around our practice (hold camera steady and level, make sure subject is in sharp focus, etc.) and then breaking them intentionally so that we can see afresh—to behave "as if the old dominant ideas no longer exist." The result, he says, will be "happy accidents" that show us things in a new way.

So I began playing with depth of field (what's in focus and what's not). I tried using black and white to tell the story and then switched to color when the landscape was largely monochromatic. I held the camera at an angle that was not the same as the subject's angle in real life and focused in an abstract fashion on nonobvious points of interest of the ice-covered object.

Perhaps Patterson's insights are a way to do what Emily Dickinson calls "telling it slant":

Tell all the Truth but tell it slant—
Success in Circuit lies
Too bright for our infirm Delight
The Truth's superb surprise
As Lightning to the Children eased
With explanation kind
The Truth must dazzle gradually
Or every man be blind—

I know that sometimes I've seen God's story for so long from one perspective—mine!—that I need to see it sideways before I recognize its power anew. Do your ideas about God's story ever keep you from refocusing? J. B. Phillips wrote an important book titled *Your God Is Too Small*. He's right. Often our God, or our view of God at least, is too small. That limited view limits our understanding of God at work in us and the world. It keeps us from seeing "all the Truth."

The first step in refocusing is to relax. There is no small irony in my writing this sentence; I am Mr. Unrelaxed. (Sigh.) Refocusing is not about trying harder in the same old ways. Refocusing is learning to relax so that we are open to seeing God at work in new ways. When we relax, we see new details—things that may have always been there but which we failed to notice because we were so focused on what we thought we should be seeing.

The second step in refocusing is getting the focus off of us and our ideas and on to what is important. This includes God, who is of Ultimate Importance. We switch ourselves off so we can switch the subject on. The subject, we soon discover, is paying attention to the eternal.

As I relaxed and took the focus off of what I thought was important, I finally was gifted by some photographs that worked to tell the story as I wanted it told. Striving did not get them. Relaxing into them did. They captured both the emotion and the wonder of the scene in such a way that I could help others experience it themselves, without me trying to describe it in words. They could behold the power and beauty, as well as other emotions that would come from their soul's experience of the photograph.

As you think about refocusing, relax your body and mind,

breathe deeply, and think slowly, gently and soulfully about the following:

- Have I set aside a time today of deep looking for God?

- Where did I see God at work (or play) in the things that went right—or wrong?

- How was God at work in the ordinary activities and experiences of my life today?

- Where should I have taken time to reframe and/or refocus?

In learning to reframe and refocus, we become like photographer Jan Phillips, who says, "My eyes find God everywhere, in every living thing, creature, person, in every act of kindness, act of nature, act of Grace."

WHAT'S THE STORY? A SPIRITUAL EXERCISE

Freeman Patterson's idea that if we want to really see we must let go of self is true for real spiritual seeing too. We can begin the process of letting go of ourselves by asking some questions that Patterson has developed as photography exercises and applying them to our lives.

As you think about your day (or week or month or life), how would you answer Patterson's questions (slightly reframed)? Reflect on the prompts in light of what you thought (as in "I thought the theme of my day was . . .") as opposed to what it really was, as you reframe and refocus it. Complete the following:

- The theme of my day was . . .

- The subject matter was . . .

- The subject matter expressed the greater theme by . . .

- What was positive was . . .

- What I learned was . . .

We often say, "Do you see what I'm getting at?" Reframing and refocusing teach us to see God at work in what we're looking at. That's something that has often gone unnoticed, if not completely unseen.

4

REFLECTING GLORY

by Beth

So all of us who have had that veil removed
can see and reflect the glory of the Lord.

2 CORINTHIANS 3:18

One fall night around dusk, I took a walk in a nature preserve near our home. As I turned onto a path that lay beside a lake, I immediately noticed the spectacular glass-like surface of the water vividly reflecting the trees, clouds and setting sun behind and above it. It was a stunning sight! I stopped, as though consecrating the moment, and studied the image of the rouge sunset, billowy clouds and tall, stalk-like trees shimmering on the water's façade. It was like seeing double—one image a mirror likeness of the other.

Even though reflections are a common phenomenon, this one had a supernatural quality. When I saw it, it appeared as an optical illusion—a mirage-like, iridescent twin vision. I was curious to understand exactly what I was seeing. As I did some reading, I learned that the reflection I saw was produced by light rays from the sun streaking down through the sky, clouds and trees (called the angle of incidence) and reflecting off the lake at the same angle (called the angle of reflection), producing a mirror image. Explainable, yet still remarkable.

The Bible tells of another extraordinary reflection, one that appeared on Moses' face. After spending time in the presence of God on Mount Sinai, Moses' face began to glow with the pure radiance of God (Exodus 34:29-35). In fact, his face became so radiant that he had to put a veil over it so as not to frighten the Israelites. When he gazed at glory, he became glorious. Paul referred to this mysterious incident in 2 Corinthians 3:18: "So all of us who have had that veil removed can see and reflect the glory of the Lord." *See* and *reflect*. What Moses and Paul tell us is that when we see God's glory, we reflect his glory.

The Bible uses the word *glory* to describe that which reflects the unique and consummate, truly beautiful nature of God. It isn't an easy concept to wrap our minds around, but when we see it, we know it. Think of a time when you noticed something extraordinary that reminded you of God and invoked a feeling of awe—a newborn's face, a brilliant sunset, a pristine lake. That's glory. Seeing glory changes us.

James Elkins, in his book *The Object Stares Back: On the Nature of Seeing,* says, "Seeing alters the thing that is seen and transforms the seer. Seeing is metamorphosis, not mechanism." When we see the divine in something, when we recognize the Creator in it, it changes what we are beholding. It is no longer an inanimate object but a mirror of God. In the process of peering into this mirror, we change as well—touched deeply by the presence and goodness of the One who created and inhabits it. Where do you find such mirrors of God today?

GLORY ON DISPLAY

Right now I am sitting in a wooded alcove in my garden. Several years ago I was inspired to create a contemplative space where I could rest and be with God. I chose this spot because of three trees that form a semicircle. Their arrangement felt sacred to me. So I cleared the ground and tamped it, set bricks and planted hostas, and purchased and placed in it a freestanding swing. This is where I come to read, meditate and talk with God during the warm months of the year.

It's about 9:30 in the morning. The sun is at a seventy-five degree angle above me, shining brilliantly through the trees. I see light rays sparkling on the leaves, reflecting off their surface—a display of unveiled beauty. What I see illumines my sense of God the Creator. The foliage acts as a mirror, shimmering with the enchantment of the morning sun. I can *see* the glory of God. My face is glowing.

This morning I am aware of my Creator in the sunlight glittering on the leaves. God's otherness and nearness touch me through the natural splendor of this setting. This experience of witnessing the glory of God changes me. It stirs a reverence for God within me. It bolsters my sense of God around me. It reminds me of who God is and what God is like—a lover of beauty, a God whose mercies are new each morning, a God who is pure as light. Perhaps like nowhere else, the glory of God is on display throughout the natural world.

That was Paul's argument to the church in Rome. He said, "For ever since the world was created, people have seen the earth and sky. Through everything God made, they can clearly see his invisible qualities—his eternal power and divine nature. So they have no excuse for not knowing God" (Romans 1:20). In fact, in the Celtic Christian tradition, the creation is referred to as God's Big Book—an expansive text of revelation, accessible to all. This distinction does not diminish the significance of the Bible, but acknowledges that no volume of words can fully contain the extraordinary and far-reaching essence of God. (For that matter, even creation is a "dim mirror.") Yet the natural world speaks persuasively of the Creator whose mind and power have no limits to conceive and produce works of art that are unparalleled. When we notice and meditate on the glory of God displayed in creation, it transforms us. We see glory and begin to reflect glory.

A TWO-WAY MIRROR

Saint Francis was drawn to Christ through seeing God's glory in creation. According to Richard Rohr,

> Nature was a mirror of the soul for St. Francis of Assisi—a mirror for himself and a mirror for God. All this mirroring affected a complete change of consciousness in how he saw reality. When Francis was a young man, he just loved to party. One night he left the party and looked up at the stars above Assisi. He stood there for a long time, and he was in awe of what he saw. He said, "If these are the creatures, what must the Creator be like?" The outer world began to name the inner experience and the nature of God for Francis. It all became a two-way mirror through which he could see God and also see his deepest soul.

The natural world is one of the most accessible places we discover the glory of God and undergo a metamorphosis. Unfortunately, we spend most of our lives holed up inside homes and offices, stores and restaurants, under fluorescent lights and in air conditioning—rarely engaging our souls with that which has the capacity to draw us into transforming worship.

In the following exercise, your mission will be to discover a sacred space—similar to my garden spot—where you can gather yourself into God's presence, see his glory and allow that glory to transform you.

SEEKING SACRED SPACE: A SPIRITUAL EXERCISE

We often have an affinity for certain bends in the road that speak to us of God's glory. Your exercise today is to find a place like that. It will involve getting up and out—taking a leisurely walk in a park or natural setting or finding a window in your home, your office or a public building (libraries and museums are great choices!) with an alluring view. As you seek this place of divine encounter, look for a serene, beautiful vista that draws you—a place that attracts and makes you feel at peace. Once you have identified a potential spot, take some time to linger. How does it feel sacred? Do you have a heightened awareness of God as you look around, observing the light and the arrangement of the scene? (If not, keep looking until you find a place where you have a strong sense of the divine.)

Once you find a view, sit and ponder your surroundings for several minutes. Allow your eyes to feast on the scene, noticing the reflections of light and all the details of the created world around you. Drink in the glory. Don't overthink what you are doing; get lost in the beauty and loveliness of the spot.

Here are a few things you can journal about or do in order to remember your time:

- Do you have a sense of God in this place? Describe what it is like.

- How is God reflected in this place? What does it tell you about him?

- As a two-way mirror, what do you see of God and what do you see of the deepest parts of your soul?

- How are you changed as you see God's glory in this place?

- Sketch what you see or take a photograph of it.

- Choose a memento from this sacred space—a leaf, rock, piece of bark, stick or feather. Place it where you can see it and be reminded of the glory of your Creator.

5

GOING OFF GRID

by Brent

One looks, one longs, and the world comes in.

JOSEPH CAMPBELL

One Saturday morning I walked into the living room to find Nancy washing windows. I almost turned around and walked back out because in this house, that's a lot of windows. We designed our home, tucked back against the woods, to get as much light inside as possible. Of course, besides letting light in, the windows afford us magnificent views.

As part of the aesthetics, we chose removable grids that make the windows look a little more barn-like (we live in a Yankee Barn home). Instead of vast sheets of glass, with the grids in place it looks like we have hundreds of little panes.

These grids, though, do something I really hadn't noticed until Nancy started washing windows. When she took the grids out, a completely new vista opened. Our living room windows stretch more than half the width of the living room and reach almost two-and-a-half stories high. With nothing in the way, the view was amazing. Though I look out that set of windows every day, I saw the woods and creek below in a fresh way. The grids have stayed out almost a year now, and I often find myself standing in front of those wide windows and enjoying the view.

SEEING CLEARLY

What sort of sights feed your soul? How do you think a shift in your point of view or perspective might change or enhance them? True sight requires attention and practice. It's more than just opening our eyes and glancing around. It's more like opening our eyes and peering deeply and pondering what's coming into our brains and souls through our eyes. This is a depth of seeing that's beyond the ordinary. It's taking a really good look.

Think of all the people you see during an average day. When someone you know comes into view, your sight shifts to them and you see them more deeply than you've seen the other folks your eyesight fell upon. Artist Alex Grey says, "In the act of deeply seeing, we transcend the boundaries between the self and the otherness of the world, momentarily merging with the thing seen." When we take a really deep look, the gulf between us and what we're looking at disappears, and we become one with what we're looking at. It becomes part of us and we become part of it. You know that is true when you see a person you love enter a room—your eyes meet and you become one with them. Thinking that way about deep seeing instills it with an intimacy that usually does not occur. But that sort of deep experience is one where life and love and God break through into our souls and bless us.

Deep seeing, as Alex Grey calls it, also merges us with God. That's because it connects us to the Divine with both attention and love. We slowly learn, by "practice seeing," that there is sublime beauty in everything around us. That includes the face of a beloved friend or the golden-lit field stubble left after harvest or a narrow city alley, swept clean by a fast-moving storm and lighted afresh by a setting sun reflected off a neighbor's window. In the act of merely thinking of clearing the grids and opening our vistas to attention and love, we begin to see that the ordinary things of our lives are sights of a spiritual beauty that lead us within sight of the Divine. We behold God's redemptive love at work in ordinary beauty.

BLOCKED VIEW

We all have a view. Each is scenic in its own way. My view is towering sycamores; for you it might be a soaring city vista or a cozy, comfortable living room filled with books, knickknacks or people you love. How do you describe your view? As you think of how the grids blocked my view, take a look around at your space. Do you see everything clearly? Or are there grids, either literal or metaphoric, that keep you from seeing all that there is? What can you clear away, at least for a time, that would open up the scene for you so that you could drink it in completely?

Enjoying the view is enough at one level. After all, I could stand in front of my windows and gaze out in deep appreciation of all that I am seeing. If I did that, my eyes would take in all sorts of things that God has provided and that bless me. But as my friend Marcy often says, I think too much. About everything. So, shortly after the grids came out, I began wondering, *Have I put up decorative grids that limit my view?* I mused on what things I needed to remove so that I could have a clearer view of my life with God.

That's not a thought uniquely my own. Christ-followers throughout history have pondered that proposition and dealt with it in a variety of ways. Some eliminated all the trappings of their lives and moved to sit atop cacti in the desert so that they would have an unobstructed view of God. Others divested themselves of all rites and rituals that they felt kept them from beholding the wonder of God. Some moved behind monastery or convent walls so that they could clearly see the Divine. Today, some people go on retreats or pilgrimages or sit in silence.

As I thought of those others who have sought a clear view of Christ, I knew I wasn't called to move to a monastery or climb a cactus. Still, I did ask:

- What things in my life are like the grids—nice, but not needed?

- What good religious things in my life need to be examined to see if they help me see God or are blocking my view?

- Which of those should be removed? And maybe left out for a good while until my vision clears?

TAKING THE SHORT VIEW: A SPIRITUAL EXERCISE

Most of the time people tell us to take the long view—to look ahead. That is not bad advice. But if that's all we do, we can miss what's right in front of us. As I discovered that Saturday morning, in my case, what was right in front of me were the window grids. I knew they were there, but I didn't really see them. They became something I looked through—the foreground that became un-noticed background. My eyes and brain had made the grids al-most invisible.

That happened to me a lot when as a young photographer I shot through things like window screens or chainlink backstops at ball games. As I focused on the scene beyond these things, the camera seemed to ignore them—until I got the pictures back, that is (those were predigital days!). Then I noticed subtle blurs where the screen or backstop was present. The blurs were out of focus, but blocked the true view.

That's what looking through the grids was like. Gazing through them made parts of the scenery outside invisible, divided by little wooden lines as it was. I couldn't see the forest for the grids. But since I didn't see what was blocking my view, I had no idea how they divided my sight until they were gone.

Part of seeing deeply (like taking a good picture) is learning not to look through obstructions. As you practice deep seeing, try tak-ing the short view first. Look for what's in the way of your long view. Is there anything in the foreground that will distort or ruin the picture?

Take a few minutes to look around you, reflecting on these questions:

- Are there things where you are sitting that you look through and don't notice?
- What would you see if you removed those things?

Next, shift your focus, literally and figuratively, from your physical surroundings to your spiritual life.

- What things block your view?
- Are there things present (maybe even good things) that keep you from seeing that which God is trying to show you?

Open your view so that, no matter where you look with longing, God will come in.

6

I SEE THE MOON

by Beth

When I look at the night sky and see the work of your fingers—
the moon and the stars you set in place—
what are mere mortals that you should think about them,
human beings that you should care for them?

PSALM 8:3-4

I grew up as a privileged child—but not in the way you might think. I was fortunate in that during my childhood, life moved slower. Summers were longer and kids played outside all day until well past dark. We had an expansive yard, almost an acre. It was a corner lot with a creek along the back and a bridge that went over the creek on one side. My most vivid memories are of sitting in the tall grasses that sloped down from the bridge, watching praying mantises; walking alongside the creek, following schools of minnows and catching tadpoles and crawdads; and at nighttime, after playing a rousing game of midnight ghost, peering up into the night sky and looking at the moon.

Then the strangest thing would happen.

I would peer at the moon, sometimes full, sometimes a crescent; sometimes clear, sometimes partially concealed by wispy clouds. I would gaze at the moon and I would swear that Someone was looking back at me.

Seeing the moon was one of my first memorable "God moments." I wasn't raised in a church-going, spiritually oriented home. I don't recall God as a subject of conversation—ever. But when I noticed the moon in the night sky and took a long, pensive look, it heightened my awareness of a transcendent Being. I often got the eerie feeling that this Being was looking back at me.

After I grew up, began my spiritual journey in earnest and had kids of my own, I read them the following poem, "I See the Moon":

I see the moon.
The moon sees me.
God bless the moon
And God bless me.

Sometimes when we looked up into the night sky, we would spontaneously recite it together, like a prayer. Seeing the moon still makes me feel like a child. When I stare up into the darkness of night and see this incandescent globe, it has a humbling effect. Like David the psalmist, I query, "When I look at the night sky and see the work of your fingers—the moon and the stars you set in place—what are mere mortals that you should think about them, human beings that you should care for them?" (Psalm 8:3-4).

Seeing the moon helps us become childlike again—a requirement, Jesus said, if we want to cross the threshold into God's kingdom come to earth. The moon has a peculiar way of evoking awareness of God and amazement at his awareness of us. As we gaze at the largeness of this brilliant luminary, we come to accept our human limitations and experience the thrilling sensation of being seen.

JAMAIS VU

There is a name for this kind of seeing the moon. You've heard the term *déjà vu*. Well, there's a different kind of experience called *jamais vu*. It describes the impression of seeing something for the first time, despite rationally knowing that you have seen this "something" many times before—like when you don't recognize a word, person or place *at first,* even though you already know it. This experience is sometimes associated with certain types of amnesia and epilepsy.

Jamais vu can happen with anything. Suddenly you see something or someone in an objective light and observe them with a new awareness and appreciation. Rob Bell, in his book *Velvet Elvis,* described this kind of moment with some friends—individuals who professed no personal faith—who were getting married. They were sitting together on a cliff overlooking a beautiful lake. He asked them why they wanted to be married in such an exquisite but remote setting. They talked about how they had fallen in love in this part of the state. Then the groom stammered, "Something holds this all together." He experienced *jamais vu*—seeing the lake and surroundings in a new way, naming the invisible witness of a transcendent Being in them. Rob then asked, "'Do you think whatever it is that holds all *this* together is the same thing that has brought you two together?' They said yes. Same thing." And they consented to call this thing "God."

When we step back and moon gaze, as if seeing this nocturnal light for the first time, we open our eyes to that "something" that holds this all together. We notice the immensity of the moon's ebony backdrop, the hundreds of thousands of miles of space between it and us, and then unexpectedly, we become conscious that the moon's Creator knows us, sees us and desires a relationship with us. We are humbled by how big it is and how small we are in the grand scheme of things. And we stammer, "What are mere mortals that you should think about them, human beings that you should care for them?"

SEEING AND BEING SEEN

What I called "God moments" as a child I now call transcendent moments. (Sounds like something an adult would say.) I like the word *transcendent* because it refers to experiences where we become uniquely aware of God—his attributes that inspire or move us, the stuff that makes God unlike anyone or anything else in the universe. In those moments, we stop in our tracks, take a deep breath and feel the connection we have with God—a God who sees us. It's not uncommon to get a lump in our throat, a shiver down our spine or a tear in our eye because we see afresh just how amazing and astonishing God truly is.

As a child, with little instruction about or exposure to concepts of God, I would look up at the moon, sense the wonder of heaven and get the peculiar feeling that God was looking back at me. The immensity of outer space overwhelmed me. The moon magnetized me. I instinctively knew that Someone created what I saw—someone who was bigger than all of it, yet aware enough, personal enough to notice me. That's how I *still* feel when I look at the moon. It has a distinctive way of cultivating my sense of God and my sense of being seen by God.

Perhaps it's because nighttime is a wonderfully contemplative occasion. Something about the quiet, enveloping darkness makes us want to stop and ponder our lives. When we look up, we are drawn by the dramatic contrast of the moon's light (reflected from the sun) against the blackness of night. The vast space, the glow of the moon and the halo around its sphere attract our attention and cause us to pause.

Even the moon's ever-changing appearance enhances our awareness of God's presence conducting the days and seasons of life. At night, unconsciously, we look for the moon's location to see whether its shape is full or partial. Its visible form changes by degrees over the month, as does its position in the night sky throughout the seasons. The moon's diminishing and expanding, its changing placement above the horizon, subtly remind us of the rhythms and forward motion of life. Seeing the moon helps us experience our inextricable connection to the sway of the universe and the God who rocks us in its sway.

The moon is also reminiscent of God because of its constancy amidst an irregular life. Like the morning sun, its nightly presence adds dependability to our shifting days. However, one of the beauties of the moon is the fact that we can stare at it for as long as we like—unlike the sun, which will blind us. We feel comfort as we contemplate the moon because we sense its stability and permanence. One of the psalmists described the sun, moon and stars as emblems of God's ardent and faithful love:

Give thanks to him who made the heavenly lights—
His faithful love endures forever.
the sun to rule the day,
His faithful love endures forever.
and the moon and stars to rule the night.
His faithful love endures forever. (Psalm 136:7-9)

Sitting under the rule of the moon's light is like finding shelter under the canopy of God's dependable love. When we take time to see it, the moon reminds us that we live in a world that God nurtures.

Hagar, an Old Testament character, had an experience of seeing the God who sees us. She was Sarai's servant and ran away after

Sarai mistreated her. She fled to the desert where the angel of the Lord found her and spoke hopeful words to her: "Thereafter, Hagar used another name to refer to the LORD, who had spoken to her. She said, 'You are the God who sees me.' She also said, 'Have I truly seen the One who sees me?'" (Genesis 16:13).

It's a moving experience to see the God who sees us. I invite you to take some time to contemplate the moon and discover its revelatory ability to help you encounter God, the God Hagar named El Roi, "the Living One who sees me" (Genesis 16:14).

MOON GAZING: A SPIRITUAL EXERCISE

Tonight or for several nights—even for thirty days—make a point to go outside or look through a window and study the moon. See it and let it see you. Feel how it feels to see the moon against the enormousness of the night sky. As you ponder the moon, notice what you observe; notice what you feel and where your thoughts are led. Talk with God, easily and naturally, like a child. Speak the name El Roi as you pray. Sit and be. If you want, take a photograph or draw a picture of the moon. Journal about your experience.

Part Three

Touch

Art Reflection on Touching

As you look at the illustration, take time to relax your body and mind. Breathe deeply. Think about the following questions slowly and gently as you look at this drawing. Savor each thought and each sensory experience that comes to you.

As you study this image of a person forming a clay vessel on a potter's wheel, what do you notice? What stands out to you?

Do you think this person has done this before? Why or why not?

What would this person's left hand feel? What would his or her right hand feel?

Notice the left thumb touching the right hand. How are the hands relating to each other? How does that help the potter touch and form the clay?

Imagine the level of pressure the potter is applying to the vessel. How would you describe it?

If you were this person, what other senses would be awakened as you formed the pot? Describe them.

How are you inspired by this image? What does it make you want to do or touch?

The Work of God's Hands (Isaiah 64:8) *is the title of this illustration. Have you ever felt God's hands shaping you? How, physically, did that feel?*

As you imagine God's hands, what do they feel like?

1

INTRODUCTION

by Beth

As the sun went down that evening, people throughout the village
brought sick family members to Jesus. No matter what their
diseases were, the touch of his hand healed every one.

LUKE 4:40

Fascinating and heartbreaking stories of feral children—children who grew up in isolation—abound. Some arise in fanciful tales like Mowgli in Rudyard Kipling's *Jungle Book*. Others surface from history books, as in the case of Victor, a twelve-year-old boy who emerged from the woods in Southern France in 1800. Even movies tell the stories of caught-in-the-wild children, like *Nell*, a 1994 film starring Jodie Foster, who lived in a primitive condition akin to feral environments. We know convincingly from these stories that a human being's health and well-being are inextricably connected to his or her exposure to loving, human touch.

With rare exception, feral children grow into adults who are unable to learn language, establish relationships and develop normal intelligence. So stunted by the absence of affection and human contact, these individuals behave more like wild animals than human beings. Even in cases where rehabilitation is attempted, feral children simply are not able to overcome the impact of growing up in a touchless world.

AN EXTRAORDINARY SENSE

Touch, an extraordinary sense, is often underappreciated and, now more than ever, viewed with extreme caution. (There is good reason to be careful because of the prevalence of child molestation. However, new safeguards can cause even appropriate touch to seem risky.) Yet it is a powerful, primal sense that protects, nurtures and forms bonds between us. We need touch to help us navigate through life—to avoid being burned by a hot stove or cut by a sharp piece of glass. We need to be touched to thrive—to develop our full mental, emotional and social intelligence. We also need touch to establish healthy relationships, to bond with others and maintain a sense of belonging.

Our sense of touch is unique to other senses. While sight, smell, taste and hearing are located in specific parts of the body, our sense of touch emanates from our entire body through our largest organ, our skin. Within the layers of our skin are tiny nerve endings that relay information about the things with which we come in contact. These receptors send information to the brain, via the spinal cord, where the feeling is registered—information about hot, cold, sharp, soft, gentle or firm.

Our sense of touch never turns off; it is constantly operating, helping us explore our world, educating us about the nature of things. Early on, we relentlessly use touch to investigate our surroundings. As we grow, we learn to interpret touch, as in the difference between a sibling's friendly joust and a forceful shove. We learn that we can cut paper and it can cut us! I remember as a young child discovering what happens if you touch the metal prongs on a toaster plug when you stick it in the socket—something I learned never to do again!

Beyond the mechanics of our sense of touch, we also receive emotional information, which conveys to our subconscious that we are safe, valued, cared for and loved by another. This message is not only meaningful, it is essential for our development. Numerous studies have shown that children who are (appropriately) held, hugged, caressed and kissed enjoy better health and growth and are more intelligent than those kept at a "cold distance." In fact, touch is so powerful that scientists believe newborns might be able to *feel* the love in a parent's touch before they feel the touch itself.

Touch is also healing. The caress of another person releases hormones in us that can ease pain and calm us down. (No wonder massage therapy has become a popular treatment for stress, chronic pain and loneliness.) Being touched lowers our blood pressure and heart rate. In fact, hands have a uniquely powerful ability to touch. The human hand possesses a refined sense of touch; each fingertip can detect a dot just three microns high. This remarkable sensitivity is attributed to the nearly two thousand touch receptors that reside on the tip of each of our fingers. We reach out to touch someone or something with our hands because no other body part (except perhaps the tongue) can feel what we touch as acutely.

THE BOND FORMED BY HUMAN TOUCH

Touch serves us well. It informs us about our world, protects us from things that can injure us and transmits emotional messages that are critical to our well-being. Touch even establishes bonds with others that deepen and enhance relationships. The University of Minnesota staged an experiment to understand the impact of touch on the relationships of perfect strangers. They placed a quarter in a phone booth at a busy intersection and watched people enter the booth to make a call. (This happened before the advent of cell phones!) They watched to see if people would pick up the quarter and use it to make their call. Invariably, they did.

Then the researcher would walk up to the person exiting the phone booth and ask if he or she had seen a quarter in the phone booth. Only 23 percent said yes and returned a quarter. After that, they repeated the experiment, only this time the researcher walked up to the person exiting the phone booth, nonchalantly *touched* the person's elbow, and asked if he or she had seen the quarter they left behind. This time, 68 percent of the people said yes and returned the quarter. Something profound happens when human beings touch! Energy is transmitted. An invisible bond is formed. We become personal to each other. We touch the humanity in another, and that makes it harder to remain indifferent.

TOUCHING JESUS

Throughout Jesus' public ministry, he touched people and they touched him. His followers "begged him to let the sick touch at least the fringe of his robe, and all who touched him were healed" (Matthew 14:36). When he returned from the grave in his resurrection body, he said to the disciples, "Look at my hands. Look at my feet. You can see that it's really me. Touch me and make sure that I am not a ghost, because ghosts don't have bodies, as you see that I do" (Luke 24:39). One evening, he went to Simon Peter's home and healed his mother-in-law of a high fever: "As the sun went down that evening, people throughout the village brought sick family members to Jesus. No matter what their diseases were, the touch of his hand healed every one" (Luke 4:40).

No matter what their diseases—communicable or incommunicable—Jesus touched them with his hands to heal them. Without the touch of Jesus, we can live our spiritual lives as though we are feral children—stunted by lack of nurture from the One who heals us and gives us life. Left to ourselves, we learn survival techniques that keep up the appearances of Christian growth and maturity. But our hearts are starved for his touch, his embrace—the One who alone loves us purely and perfectly. So how can we experience the touch of Jesus today?

Some Christian traditions have an advantage over others. Incorporated in their liturgy or worship times are kinesthetic experiences like touching the cross, kissing an icon, dipping fingers in the baptismal water—elements that provide a sensory connection with Jesus, the invisible yet present One. In the following exercise, you will be invited to touch Jesus and allow him, in turn, to touch you. Through your sense of touch, may you feel his presence and bond with him more deeply.

TOUCHING JESUS: A SPIRITUAL EXERCISE

Choose a sacred object that is symbolic of Christ. You might select a cross, a crucifix, a rock, a chalice of wine, a picture of Jesus, a rosary or a Bible. Choose something through which you feel drawn to Jesus, and that is comfortable to hold in your hands.

- Hold this object in your hands. Feel it, exploring the shape, texture, temperature and composition. How does it feel to you? What about it reminds you of Jesus? Use all your senses to explore it.

- As you hold it in your hands, what do you feel compelled to do with it? Kiss it? Raise it up toward heaven? Hold it close to your heart?

- Say the Lord's Prayer as you hold and feel your sacred object:
    Our Father in heaven,
        may your name be kept holy.
    May your Kingdom come soon.
    May your will be done on earth,
        as it is in heaven.
    Give us today the food we need,
    and forgive us our sins,
        as we have forgiven those who sin against us.
    And don't let us yield to temptation,
        but rescue us from the evil one.

- As you touch this sacred object, imagine touching Jesus—his face, his heart, his nail-pierced hands.

- Imagine Jesus placing his hands on your head or shoulders. Hear him pray a prayer of blessing over you. What do you hear him say?

2

TEXTURES

by Brent

And you also were included in Christ when you
heard the message of truth, the gospel of your salvation. Having be-
lieved, you were marked in him with a seal, the promised Holy Spirit.

EPHESIANS 1:13 (NIV)

I taught Sunday School recently. That was something I vowed I would never do again after volunteering for a six-week course that turned into six years of teaching. I didn't quit; I moved to another town!

Despite my vow, I said yes when asked to teach at the congregation I attend. Some of the exercises I had the class do used flip-chart paper and colored markers. Most people seemed to enjoy the exercises. I'd like to think that was because the projects had some spiritual significance, but even if it was just that the folks got to play with markers, well, that is fine by me.

While the class was working on one assignment, I pulled out a thin pastel blue marker and made a tiny dot on my hand. I didn't do it for any reason other than wanting to see what it looked like. A friend of mine says I'm an eternal twelve-year-old. Maybe so.

When I looked hours later, the mark was still there. But it was different. The color that had been smooth and vibrant when first applied was now faded and wrinkly on my hand. It grew more faded and wrinkly as the day went by.

PRAYER TEXTURES

Textures make life interesting. We like textures in our textiles, our food, our wallpaper and rugs. While we like our roads to be smooth (and wish our metaphorical life road had been free of potholes), the fact is we are the people that we are in no small part thanks to the textures we've encountered along the way.

What are some of the textures around you right now? Smooth wood desk? Ribbed corduroy pants? Nubby chair fabric? As you look at them, pick one that represents your life right now. Run your fingers over it. As you feel that texture, what words, phrases or questions come to mind as you contemplate how it reminds you of your life?

Continue to feel it and allow other words to connect and flow out as you touch the texture. Imagine a large piece of that texture covered with the words and thoughts that have been moving through you. Then circle out from that with other words as they pop into your brain or soul.

Finally, while still feeling the texture, go into a time of prayer. Let the words and thoughts you've had flow through your fingers up into your brain and out to the mind and love of God.

Since Jesus told us we should become as little children (Matthew 18:3), look around for a marker or pen or pencil. Place a tiny dot somewhere on your skin. Allow it to remain there as long as it will to serve as a reminder of the textures of your life and God's presence in them.

ROUGH PLACES MADE SMOOTH OR
SMOOTH PLACES MADE ROUGH?

We all know the well-worn poem "Footprints" about two sets of footprints in the sand that narrow down to one. The poet asks Jesus, "I have noticed that during the most trying periods of my life there has only been one set of footprints in the sand. Why, when I needed you most, have you not been there for me?"

That may be your experience. That's not a new question—for the poet or you. It's a variation on David's, "My God, my God, why have you forsaken me? Why are you so far from saving me, so far from my cries of anguish?" (Psalm 22:1 NIV).

Or your experience may be one where you know that Jesus has carried you through the difficult times and you can say, "Every valley shall be filled in, every mountain and hill made low. The crooked roads shall become straight, the rough ways smooth" (Luke 3:5 NIV; see also Isaiah 40:3-5).

Regardless, take a few moments of silent reflection and think about God and the textures of your life by considering the following questions:

• Where is God present in them?

• Where does God feel absent?

• What would you like to ask God about the textures?

As I feel (figuratively) my life's textures, I find that, like yours, they are many. Some were smooth, like the times when I felt in complete sync with God. At those times, the marker of my life moved easily across the paper.

Others were rough, like trying to draw on a piece of sandpaper. The marker skipped and jumped and I really had to bear down to leave a mark. I think that describes some of my most obstinate times, of which there are too many.

At other times, the marker was fine, but the surface was slick. Beyond smooth, it was glossy and would not take the color. It smeared even if lightly touched. I think those were the times that I was a young know-it-all. As a young person full of college and seminary training, I had all the spiritual answers. So I really didn't need God's help in thinking things through. I had already thought them through, thank you very much. Pause for a few moments to think about the textures of your life with God.

TEXTURES OF LIFE: A SPIRITUAL EXERCISE

Look at your hand and see where you left your marker mark. I left my mark on my hand for most of the next couple of days to remind me to ponder the textures of my spiritual life. As you think about the textures of your life with God, take a few minutes and look around where you are now. Look for some markers or a pen or pencil and different types of papers. Especially look for things you wouldn't normally think of as drawing paper or a marker (for example, sandpaper, grocery bags, magazines, old bills or your hand—if you're eternally twelve like me—could all be used as paper; a tube of lipstick could serve as a writing utensil).

Begin to doodle whatever comes to mind. Don't worry about what you're doodling—just let it flow. You won't be hanging this for exhibition in the Louvre or even on your refrigerator (unless you want to). Unlike what much of our product-oriented society tells us, the goal here is not the end "product." Instead, the aim is participating in the creative, prayerful process of opening ourselves to seeing what our lives are saying to us about God and our journey to God. This is a pilgrimage with paper and pencil, a journey with the intention of encountering Christ through our bodies as well as our minds and souls.

As you draw, focus on the idea of where God is working with you (maybe even subconsciously) in the things you are drawing and the types of papers you're using.

- Do they represent your life now or in the past?
- Which seasons of your life have been smooth, rough, slick, colorful, muted?

- How do the papers you've found represent some of the textures of your life?

- How do the textures speak to you?

Don't hurry this process. Sense the texture of the paper. Notice the feel of your marking utensil. Take your time. You want to give yourself enough time (and only you can decide how much time is "enough") to completely engage with the piece you've created and to fully reflect on it.

Don't rush. You might even want to set it aside, return to it in a day or a week (or a month), and see what it says to you then.

Use your creative touch—your feeling art—to teach your soul Christ's lessons.

3

A PILE OF STONES

by Beth

*He took twelve stones, one to represent each
of the tribes of Israel, and he used the stones to
rebuild the altar in the name of the LORD.*

1 KINGS 18:31-32

I am more artist than scientist in the kitchen. That means I generally make a big mess when I cook. I don't often measure or stick to a recipe; I use instinct more than instructions; I'm sloppy, inexact and flamboyant. But over the years, I've also learned to be resourceful. I've learned to use leftovers, substitute one thing for another, and save bones for broth and scraps for soup. In fact, during my Thirty Days of Touch, I made one of my favorite soups from homemade stock—white bean chicken chili. In preparation, I stewed two whole chickens in a large pot to make the stock. After they were cooked, I spent the bulk of a half hour picking the meat off the bones. With my hands covered in grease, I sifted each part of the chicken through my fingers, dissecting the meat from the skin, joints, cartilage and bones, trying not to waste any.

I went to a good deal of trouble to extract as much as I could from the chicken, as much as was usable for the stock and the soup. My fingers ran over every millimeter of that chicken's carcass, searching and salvaging every shred of meat I could. All this trouble, all this effort, turned my thoughts toward God. As I was gleaning meat from the remains, I kept thinking about what I was touching and what it was teaching me about the ways of God.

It didn't take long before I pictured God's hands as he scavenged through the particles of my life, his fingers touching each aspect as he considered it for his purposes. I thought of how resourceful he has been over my lifetime. The things that I might have thought to be useless or disgusting, he envisioned with redemptive eyes. The experiences of my life that were, at the time, absent of good, he found a means through which to grace me. What I considered trash—moral failures, mistakes, broken relationships and wounds—has taken on a different cast in the light of his presence. I'm not suggesting that they were good in themselves. I'm saying that in spite of their repugnance, I found God leaning over the rubble, looking through the ruins and finding a way to reuse them in a soul-expanding, character-building, grace-giving way.

Here's an example from the most profoundly painful experience my husband and I have gone through. After a number of years of fruitful labor and one year of horrible conflict, we left a ministry context bleeding, hurt and angry. At the time, it was impossible to imagine that I would one day appreciate what God has done in me through the experience—not only through all the wonderful opportunities our departure has opened up, but even through the pain itself. In my anger, bitterness and sorrow, I traveled with God into a very deep, dark valley. And in that place, God began to expose and disentangle some of my false ways of being that I had developed over my lifetime. The result has freed me to grow more fully into my true self. Today I sense a deeper wholeness, congruency and confidence in who I am in Christ.

RUBBLE

God is a master at using rubble to rebuild our lives. That's what he did for me and that's what he did for Israel during the days of Elijah. Ahab was king, and Israel was in a terrible spiritual state. So Elijah called the people to Mount Carmel to witness a showdown between Yahweh and Ahab and the prophets of Baal. His enemies built an altar to their god and asked for fire from heaven to consume their altar, but none came. It was then Elijah's turn to entreat God to show the people his mighty power: "Then Elijah called to the people, 'Come over here!' They all crowded around him as he repaired the altar of the LORD that had been torn down. He took twelve stones, one to represent each of the tribes of Israel, and he used the stones to rebuild the altar in the name of the LORD" (1 Kings 18:30-32).

Imagine this: All the people gathered around this pathetic, embarrassing emblem of their own spiritual collapse—a broken, dismantled altar. And what does God instruct Elijah to do? *Rebuild* the altar, not from scratch, but with the *rubble,* with the discarded pile of stones scattered around its base. Elijah took twelve of them and built it, each to represent a tribe from whom every single Israelite claimed his or her lineage. The message couldn't be more piercing. God said to them, "I will take your own failures and infidelity and use them to rebuild a future for me and you."

REBUILDING

Anything placed in God's hands becomes a tool for rebuilding our lives. In fact, when we give over to God the things that have caused us the most pain, he turns around and uses them to forge our calling. C. S. Lewis, in a letter to Sheldon Vanauken, said that "every disability conceals a vocation, if only we can find it." Isn't it true that we are the most empathic and compassionate toward people whose issues are similar to our own? All the rubble around us, the debris that exists because of unwelcomed circumstances or deliberate choices, becomes a source used for rebuilding our lives and a tool to inform our calling.

How have you seen God take the scraps of life and turn them into resources that give life? How has he done that for you? Because of his unfailing love, he pledges to restore our lives. "I have loved you, my people, with an everlasting love. With unfailing love I have drawn you to myself. I will rebuild you" (Jeremiah 31:3-4). In the following exercise, you will identify the rubble that God has used or is using resourcefully to rebuild your life.

BUILDING YOUR OWN ALTAR: A SPIRITUAL EXERCISE

Just as God instructed Elijah to rebuild the altar from the rubble of Israel's broken relationship with him, during this exercise you will build an altar that represents the stones that God is using to reclaim your life and rebuild your future. You will need six to twelve medium-sized stones or rocks that have a surface on which you can write.

- What are the significant choices, losses, failures and hurts from your past for which you are still paying a price? Write them down and narrow them to a list no greater than your number of stones.
- Take each stone, one at a time, and hold it in your hand. Feel the weight, texture, shape, temperature and composition.

- Write on each stone a word or symbol that represents each event or issue from your list. Don't write anything that you would be uncomfortable for someone else to see. Instead, write a symbol that helps you know what that rock represents.

- Now carefully stack the rocks in a pile on your desk, bookshelf or dresser—some place where you can be visually reminded that God is rebuilding your life from the rubble.

- After you have built your altar, offer God a sacrifice of thanksgiving—not for anything abusive or traumatic, but for his grace present to you in the rubble.

- Every time you see your altar, remember to thank him for how he is redeeming the pile of stones, the rubble in your life.

4

TOUCHING ABSENCE

by Brent

Will the Lord reject us forever?
Will he show us his favor no more?
Has his love vanished forever?
Has his promise come to an end?

PSALM 77:7-8

No car key. That's what I discovered one frigid winter morning at Meeting. I arrived early, jumped out and hit the lock button on the car. Andy (my car) made a funny bleat that I chalked up to the extreme cold. Once indoors, I took off my winter togs and hat and headed to worship. As I sat in Meeting, I put my hands in my pants pockets and felt, um, nothing. No car key. Though I doubt my visage displayed any alarm, my inner eyes flew open wide, and I wondered where it could have gotten to and how in the world I'd get home if I didn't find it. I tried to let those worries go and settle into worship, but I couldn't. I felt, literally, the key's absence. Something that was always present in my pocket was not there. And I knew it wasn't because I kept touching the space where it wasn't.

Have you ever discovered something's absence by reaching for it and finding it not there? What did that feel like, both physically and emotionally? How did your body tell you it wasn't there? What *didn't* you feel?

LOST

As I sat in the gathering silence of Meeting, my continual reaching for something that was supposed to be there and feeling that it wasn't made me think of despairing times in my life when God has seemed absent. Who among us has not at some time cried with David, "My God, my God, why have you forsaken me?" (Psalm 22:1 NIV)? If not aloud, at least deep inwardly.

Many people have felt God's absence. They feel a missing-ness where something steady and dependable once was. Mother Teresa felt that absence. *Mother Teresa: Come Be My Light* is mostly a collection of letters between her, her confessors and her superiors spanning more than half a century. The letters reveal a deep, personal despairing feeling of God's absence. This inner despair stands in stark contrast to Mother Teresa's public image of a smiling saint completely at ease with her divine call to serve the poor and wretched of Calcutta. The letters show that for the last half century of her life she felt no presence of God whatsoever.

She felt this absence keenly, having known the presence of God as a life-changing constant. This steady Presence comforted her—until she felt the void, which indicated its absence. Touching the missingness revealed the loss. Like my feeling my key *not* there, she noticed the feeling of God *not* there.

Of course, Mother Teresa is not the only child of God to have felt this absence. The Reformer Martin Luther and the nineteenth-century French Carmelite Thérèse of Lisieux, among others, have written poignantly of their experiences. The Spanish mystic John of the Cross coined the phrase "dark night of the soul" to describe his feeling of God's absence.

Have you ever felt a dark night of the soul or something else that felt like God's absence? What did that absence feel like? I don't mean as an emotional or spiritual experience—I mean bodily. Think about that time. Did your body feel the absence? How did your body react to the spiritual feeling of God's absence? What did you feel? What *didn't* you feel?

FEELING AROUND

The touch of absence is not a good feeling. Still, if I had not felt the absence of the key in my pocket, I would not have started on a search. While it was not a great quest in the scheme of life, it was important if I wished to travel home after Meeting.

Likewise, the feeling of God's absence can either lead us to despair or call us to begin a search for the divine presence that gives us life. This is a search as old as humankind and that calls to us from deep in our bones and souls. As the psalmist says, "My heart says of you, 'Seek his face!' Your face, LORD, I will seek" (Psalm 27:8 NIV).

Indeed. And yet I sometimes need the nudge of absence to set me seeking God's face again. I misplace myself sometimes, like I misplaced Andy's key. I misplace myself when I forget that it is not in my own strength that I live and move and have my being.

Then a sense of God's absence comes. So I begin seeking and searching—sometimes frantically.

Have you felt hungry to reconnect with the touch of divine power? What were you feeling when you knew you had the need to touch, or be touched, by God? What were the clues—either bodily or spiritually? How did you begin feeling around? Were you ever surprised by what you felt?

I am, sometimes. I think that's how God works—through divine surprises. I find something completely different from what I thought I was looking for. As I sat in worship touching the empty space in my pants pocket where my key should have been, I thought I was trying to remember where that key was. And, at one level, I was. But as I mused about the key and its missingness, I realized that I was really looking for so much more. The key I really needed that morning was not a literal fob stamped with the Toyota corporate emblem. The thing I was really searching for, the key, was time with the God who, as Paul says, "set his seal of ownership" on me (2 Corinthians 1:22 NIV). That's because God is the key that gives me life. Indeed, as Paul told the people of Athens:

> The God who made the world and everything in it is the Lord of heaven and earth and does not live in temples built by human hands. And he is not served by human hands, as if he needed anything. Rather he himself gives everyone life and breath and everything else. From one man he made all the nations, that they should inhabit the whole earth; and he marked out their appointed times in history and the boundaries of their lands. God did this so that they would seek him and perhaps reach out for him and find him, though he is not far from any one of us. (Acts 17:24-27 NIV)

As I thought about that, I asked myself some questions:

- What is it about God that animates me?

- How, in tangible ways, does God give me life and breath and everything else?

That I needed to take time to reconnect with the truths behind those questions was what the touch of absence taught me that morning.

Oh, and I did find the key. It had fallen out of my pocket and was lying on the floor between the driver's seat and console.

TOUCHING ABSENCE: A SPIRITUAL EXERCISE

Since it is God who gives us life, breath and everything else, it's no wonder we find the feeling of God's absence so disturbing. Since it is in God that we live and move and have our being, feeling God's absence is the feeling of death and despair. The dark night of the soul, indeed. The dark night of no life.

Until recent times, the people of God often were more in touch with their bodies and allowed them to be used as spiritual teaching tools. This includes the sense of touch. The Bible is filled with references of people who are in mourning or repentant wearing sackcloth. While, when we hear that word, we may think of a garment made out of an old burlap sack, a sackcloth garment was actually made out of coarse animal (often goat) hair. Worn against the skin, it was meant to cause discomfort to remind the wearer to be repentant. Sackcloth is the origin of the hair shirt that was used in some religious traditions until fairly recently.

I am not suggesting wearing a hair shirt or sackcloth, but as you think of God's absence, consider the following:

- What cloth, if you wore it, would feel like God's absence to you? Why?
- What other textures feel like God's absence?
- What thing, when you do not feel it where it should be, feels like God's absence?

5

FEELING YOUR PRAYERS

by Beth

I pray that . . . Christ will make his home in your hearts
as you trust in him. Your roots will grow down
into God's love and keep you strong.

EPHESIANS 3:16-17

We've lived in our home for fourteen years—the longest of any home during our marriage. By this time, we've worn traffic patterns in the carpet, replaced a roof from hail damage, painted and repainted. We've raised four kids in this home, who rotated bedrooms throughout different periods in their childhood and adolescence. We've had two dogs during our stint. Butter, our yellow lab, lived and died here—after chewing a number of holes in the drywall that have now been patched and repainted. Bongo, dog number two—a quirky Australian shepherd with one blue and one brown eye—has been with us for five years. He's made his home in every room, on any piece of furniture he pleases, and he makes coming home a jubilant reentry.

Our history in this home provides a wonderful, familiar comfort. It doesn't matter if I've been gone for a few hours, a day or a week; when I come home, I am awash with deep gladness as if being greeted by a large-bosomed grandma who wraps her arms around me and gives me a big squeeze. I've come home. My heart knows it. I've come home, and my body sinks right into the fabric and flow of this blessed place we've made our home.

What does it feel like to you to come home?

Our lives need to come and go from home. We come home from a day's work, go to bed, wake up the next morning and go back out into the world. We leave home and take trips for work, vacations and visits. When our traveling is over, we return home. We move away from our childhood home and make other homes our home. And when we return to our original habitat, it's as though we've clicked the channel of our memory to a rerun that we know by heart but had not thought of over the months and years away. Home seeps into the deepest part of our being; it has a permeating, anchoring and formative effect on us.

Just as we experience repeated coming and going from our physical homes, we likewise experience the same movement in our spiritual lives. At times, we are drawn inward toward a contemplative period of deeper self-awareness followed by nudges from the Spirit to move outward, toward life, important work and connections with others. Coming home and going out, this journey inward and journey outward, is a natural rhythm in our spiritual lives. Our sense of touch helps rehearse this movement so that we keep our balance and remain rooted.

Elizabeth O'Connor, in *Journey Inward, Journey Outward*, tells the formational story of The Church of the Saviour in Washington, D.C.—a church that is innovative, philosophically and missionally. O'Connor says, "While it is a crucial mistake to assume that churches can be on an outward journey without being on an inward one, it is equally disastrous to assume that one can make the journey inward without taking the journey outward." She explains that these opposing movements must always be held in tension within our individual lives and within the church. Both are essential for wholeness and living in God's purposes and are nurtured through three critical engagements:

- engagement with oneself
- engagement with God
- engagement with others

ENGAGEMENT WITH ONESELF

Coming home to oneself is critical to a healthy, growing life in God. To come home, we must become self-aware and acknowledge our true feelings and the motives operating within us. We must attend to the real questions and fears that rumble around in the basement of our hearts—a room that many of us have an aversion to. O'Conner writes, "As people on an inward journey, we are committed to growing in consciousness, to becoming people in touch with our real selves, so that we know not only what flows at the surface, but what goes on in the depths of us."

Our "real selves" or true selves are both the person we are at present and the person we have the potential to become. Being real necessitates an honest, current assessment of the issues that hold us back and the vain energies that direct much of our efforts. Being real also requires a growing knowledge of the person God created us to be—with all our possibilities and gifts. When we awaken to our true selves, when we "come home," this journey inward is what facilitates genuine transformation. Change happens when we abide in our true selves and invite Christ's Spirit to breathe life into us so that we live increasingly from that home.

ENGAGEMENT WITH GOD

Not only do we need to engage with ourselves as we respond to the flow of this inward/outward journey, we need to also engage with God. "The goal we have been speaking of here is the one of getting our lives rooted in God, so that they are not blown and tossed about by every wind. We need the engagement with self to find out that we have our houses resting on sand, but there is no possibility of getting them over on rock without an engagement with God." Because of the natural, unavoidable movements of life, we desperately need an anchor.

Jesus bid his beleaguered followers to find their home in him. He said, "Come to me, all of you who are weary and carry heavy burdens, and I will give you rest" (Matthew 11:28). Home is where we rest and are restored. Jesus told his anxious followers that he and his Father "will come and make our home with each of them" (John 14:23). Home is a place where we make relationships—where we receive and offer love. Like a firmly rooted tree that bends with the wind or flexes in a storm, we will comply best with the inward and outward movements of life when we are rooted deeply in Christ, as Paul prayed: "Christ will make his home in your hearts as you trust in him. Your roots will grow down into God's love and keep you strong" (Ephesians 3:17).

ENGAGEMENT WITH OTHERS

As much as we need moments, periods, even seasons of living contemplatively—journeying inward—those times prepare us to move out in unison with God, to collaborate with his great work in the world. Each of us has a task to do, good work to accomplish, a life to steward. When we fail to move out, to go in his power, we thwart God's plans and compromise our purpose. Yet it's common for Christians to remain homebound, retreating to church and a life that has little involvement with those different from them, those beyond their front door. Think how odd it is when you hear of a person who never leaves home—a recluse, we call them. When Christ-followers stay holed up at home, never engaging in the larger world, we become spiritual recluses.

Just as Jesus invited his followers home, he also bid them *go*. "Therefore, go and make disciples of all the nations" (Matthew 28:19). "Again he said, 'Peace be with you. As the Father has sent me, so I am sending you'" (John 20:21). Jesus draws us home to feed and clothe us. Then he sends us out to do the same for others.

FEELING YOUR PRAYERS: A SPIRITUAL EXERCISE

Sometimes we resist the tension that coming and going creates. We want to live into one without returning to the other. The following exercise, using a finger labyrinth, can help us feel our prayers as we rehearse the natural inward/outward cycle of life. A labyrinth is an ancient symbol of the ebbing and flowing of life and the necessity of inward and outward motion. It is different from a maze in that there are no dead ends, but there is always movement: inward and outward. In this exercise, you have the opportunity to pray a "coming home and going out" prayer. For nearly a year, I prayed this prayer almost daily. It became a rich rhythm that helped me sound my prayers to God as I acknowledged the internal and external journey of my life.

As you feel your prayer:

- Touch the labyrinth, moving your finger inward with each phrase of the inward prayer. Once you arrive "home," take several moments to be at home with God. Ask the Spirit to bring to mind any new revelation about you—an inner feeling you have not acknowledged or explored, a false way of being, a gift you have not recognized and fostered.

- After a time of centering, touch the labyrinth, moving outward with each phrase of the outward prayer. Ask God to open your eyes to where he wants you to go, who he wants you to meet, what he wants you to do.

JOURNEY INWARD

Gracious God, the God who woos me,
Draw me by your Spirit into silence and stillness,
Help me find my way home.
Anchor me in your love and grace
As I come to you in my weakness
And learn from your gentle and humble heart.
Give rest to my soul.

JOURNEY OUTWARD

Gracious God, the God who sends me,
Lead me by your Spirit with courage and strength,
Help me find my place in the world.
Fill me with joy from serving you
As I become your hands and feet
And learn to love as you have loved me.
Give vision to my soul.

6

TOUCHING JESUS

by Brent

Look at my hands and my feet. It is I myself! Touch me and see.

LUKE 24:39 (NIV)

I was in my usual hurry to work when I spied a big, black, evil SUV sitting in the curb lane. The no-parking lane. The lane I use to get to the parking lot. The light I approached turned red. I stopped and glared at the back end of the SUV with its brake lights gleaming a half block ahead. Just sitting there. *What a doofus, I* thought. *Now I'll either have to race ahead of the guy next to me and get in front of him, or creep through the light, wait for the line of cars on my right to pass me, and then fall in behind them and probably not make it through the next light.* Sitting there I got more and more upset with this person who was blocking my way—*my* important way—down the street.

Then just as the light changed, the big, black, evil SUV took a hard right across all four lanes of traffic and pulled into a parking spot. The driver climbed out and bounded up the steps of St. Mary Catholic Church. There he stood in front of a statue of Jesus. He reached up and began touching its face, its hair, the folds of the robe. My anger drained.

Embarrassed, I glanced in the rearview mirror as I passed. The man still stood there, touching, caressing, Jesus.

I felt foolish.

I also felt humbled. I rush by that statue every day. Sometimes I see it; most times not. But here was a man who stopped just to touch Jesus. I don't know his story. Perhaps he just wanted to see how the sculptor had formed the statue. But something tells me he had some deeper reason for that touch.

THE HEALING TOUCH

As I turned into the parking lot, I thought of the biblical story of the woman who was ill and went looking for Jesus. When she found him, after twelve years of hemorrhaging, the Bible says she "came up behind him and touched the edge of his cloak. She said to herself, 'If I only touch his cloak, I will be healed'" (Matthew 9:20-21 NIV).

"If I only touch his cloak, I will be healed." I wonder if the man in the SUV was remembering those verses? Regardless, she was right. The act of touching healed her.

What could you touch today that would bring a bit of healing to you?

Perhaps you've never even considered that question. I know I have not often thought of touching something as a way of connecting with God. I think of prayer as doing that. Or asking others to pray.

But touch?

As I pondered it, though, I realized that I know a number of people who touch God—though they may not put it quite that way—every day. One friend has a mezuzah on his office door frame. A mezuzah is a piece of parchment, often contained in a decorative case, inscribed with verses from the Torah.

Some of my Catholic, Orthodox and Anglican friends wear tiny crosses and carry prayer books or rosaries.

Those of us from nonliturgical traditions have nothing pre-scribed like that. So some of us devise our own. One friend I know carries a coin from a foreign country he visited on a mission trip. Another keeps a stone from a spiritually significant place he stayed. One carries a well-worn little book about faith and art.

All of these are spiritual forms and forces reinforced by touch.

Feel around. Is there something close to you, in your pocket or hanging nearby, that you touch to connect to God? It might be something as overtly religious as a mezuzah, or it might be something informal, like the little white cut paper dove given to me by some young adult Friends. What would you use to represent the healing touch of God in your life? What are the literal touchstones of your faith?

You might need to create your own faith-piece. Even though many of us do not see ourselves as creators, we are frequently creating things—from projects at work to fresh-baked bread for our families. Each creation can be made to the glory of God. That includes making a piece to touch to remind us of the God who touches every part of our lives. Creating is holy play that opens us to God. Creating in the attitude of play and not drudgery is part of our being created in God's image. As Betsey Beckman says, "If God is creator and we are made in God's image of *Imago Dei*, then we are, in our essence, creators. We are, in our essence, artists. Therefore, when we open ourselves to the expression of creativity, we also open to the movement of the Divine within us."

Create something that opens you to the movement of God within you, something you can touch.

ENOUGH TO GO AROUND

Unlike the woman who was bleeding, there are times I don't want to bother God with my need for healing. After all, how does my bleeding soul compare to the starving children around the world? I guess I sometimes see God as a sort of Mr. Bumble from Charles Dickens's *Oliver Twist* and the musical *Oliver!* Bumble is a pompous, self-righteous church official who preaches Christian charity but does not practice it toward those under his care.

I think of myself as Oliver. Do I dare bring my petty needs to the important one? I imagine my scene of approaching God as Oliver approaches Mr. Bumble, bowl in hand:

Oliver Twist: Please sir, I want some more.

Mr. Bumble: [*thinking he must not have heard right*] What?

Oliver Twist: Please sir, I want some . . .

[*pauses hesitatingly*]

Oliver Twist: more?

Mr. Bumble: [*surprised beyond belief*] More?

When I think of God within such human constraints, especially as a Mr. Bumble type, I deny God's otherness. God is beyond us. The divine resources are unlimited. The story of the woman who came for healing also shows us that. She was not the only person who came for healing that day. Indeed, she was not even the one most in need of help, according to how we measure such things. The story opens with a ruler coming and kneeling before Jesus and pleading, "My daughter has just died. But come and put your hand on her, and she will live" (Matthew 9:18 NIV). Jesus and his disciples are setting out to this man's house when the woman reaches out to touch him.

According to the Gospels, Jesus is always touching or being touched, even after the resurrection. As Sara Miles reminds us, "In the stories of the risen Jesus, his disciples frequently think he must be a ghost. But he asks them for something to eat, he tells them to feel his side, he puts his hands on them. And then Jesus commissions his disciples, giving them the power to share in resurrection. He does it through breath and touch, through Spirit and flesh."

The touch and touching of Jesus, both fleshly and spiritually, heal both the girl and the sick woman. They heal us today. There's no need for pleading for more. There's more than enough. I need to use the imaginative soul that God gave me and rewrite the scene from *Oliver!* to be more like this:

Brent ina Twist: Please sir, I want some more.

God: Okay.

Brent ina Twist: Please sir, I want some . . .
[*pauses hesitatingly, thinking he must not have heard right*]
Brent ina Twist: more?
God: [*reaching out to touch me*] Sure. What and how much would you like?

How would you rewrite that scene for yourself? What would you like more of?

The Bible story of the woman of faith reminds us that we all could use a cure that comes from a caress. A cure for conditions that nobody but Jesus knows.

A touch.

So simple and yet so hard to remember.

THE FAITH OF TOUCH: A SPIRITUAL EXERCISE

Another thing I wonder about the woman who touched Jesus' robe is, what was it that told her soul that touching Jesus would heal her?

We don't know much about her beyond what the Bible tells us in this passage. All we really know is that she had faith that her touch would do the trick. She believed. And, according to Jesus, that was all that was needed—belief.

Matthew 9:22 tells us that "Jesus turned and saw her. 'Take heart, daughter,' he said, 'your faith has healed you.' And the woman was healed at that moment" (NIV).

I invite you to take a journey of divine imagination with me. I am not asking you to pretend. I am inviting you to live into the Bible story by placing yourself in it. Close your eyes. Take a couple of deep breaths and begin imagining you are that woman. You are weak and in dire need of healing. You hobble along to be where Jesus is.

- Do you wait or do you immediately reach a trembling hand out from deep inside your coarse cloth robe and touch his clothes?
- What do his robes feel like?

- What physical sensations do you experience?

Live into the moment.

- Can you feel the healing coursing through you?
- Can you see Jesus turn and look at you?
- What does he say? What words does he speak?
- What's his tone of voice?
- How do you know you are healed?

As you open your eyes and come back to the present, do you still feel a trace of the divine touch? Carry that feeling with you throughout the day—and "touch it" (figuratively) as a way to stay connected with God.

Part Four
Hear

Art Reflection on Hearing

Turn to the illustration that opens this chapter. As you look at it, take time to relax your body and mind. Breathe deeply. Think about the following questions slowly and gently as you look at this drawing. Savor each thought and each sensory experience that comes to you.

As you muse over this endearing picture of two children, one whispering in the other's ear, where are your eyes drawn? What stands out to you?

What do you "hear" the one child saying to the other child? Why do you suppose she is whispering?

How would you describe the way the one child is listening? What gives you clues?

What do you imagine to be the relationship between these two children? Why?

What do you think will happen next? Why?

If you were one of the children in this scene, what other senses would be awakened? Describe them.

How are you inspired by this image? What does it make you want to do or hear?

Have you ever had good news of God that you wanted to share with someone close to you? Did you whisper it, close to your friend's ear, like this little girl?

Likewise, have you ever had someone whisper good news of God in your ear? What did that feel like? Sound like?

Marcy Jean Stacey, the artist, titled this piece Tell of God's Wonderful Deeds *(Psalm 9:1). What title would you give to it? Why?*

1

INTRODUCTION

by Beth

My sheep listen to my voice; I know them, and they follow me.

JOHN 10:27

ACTIVE LISTENING

Not long ago, I had an opportunity to stretch my listening skills. I sat with a woman for nearly two hours, hearing an extensive, detailed description of her life and journey. It was hard work! Hard work to stay present with her, to not zone out and take a mental holiday somewhere else. In the midst of our conversation, I became aware of my need to pray and stay connected to God as I listened intently to her and her story. After some time, the folds of her heart began to open. Tears flowed freely, pooling in her eyes and overflowing onto her cheeks. She spoke of things that she hadn't expressed before. She articulated words that for the first time she heard her own voice speak. Thoughts that needed to come out. Pain that needed a voice. Worries that had been imprisoned and longed to be released.

As I listened, occasionally asking a question, adding a cupful of thoughts to the torrent of hers, I sensed that we had discovered holy ground together. Afterward, she hugged me tight and thanked me for listening, as if I'd offered her some extraordinary gift. She expressed to me how much it meant to be heard. I later pondered why conversations like that one are so rare. Why do I seldom give another my full, undivided attention? And, for that matter, why do I so infrequently feel heard?

Our sense of hearing is a rare, sophisticated, complex gift—the collaborative efforts of our outer, middle and inner ears with our auditory nervous system. Described simply, our ears pick up sound vibrations, which are transformed into nerve impulses that travel to the brain and are interpreted based on our memory of that sound. Amazingly, we can differentiate between thousands of auditory memories. And even though our auditory radar is turned on all the time—even when we're sleeping—hearing a sound is very different from listening to it.

We hear the dryer buzz, but we don't pay attention to it and fold the clothes before they wrinkle. We hear our child say something but don't listen to an important clue about his or her day. We hear an odd sound under the car hood but tune it out and are sorry later. Just as our eyes perceive an entire field of view but can miss seeing what is before us, so our ears can detect sound yet not attend to the sound and translate what it is or what it means. Perhaps that's why we have so few conversations like the one I described earlier. We hear, but we don't always listen.

Active listening is a developed skill. It is hard work. It requires the use of our extraordinary sense of hearing, but it takes more than merely detecting sound—it requires that we focus on what we hear while blocking out peripheral noise and internal distractions, in order to discern what is being said. As a spiritual director, I have been trained in the ministry of active listening, helping a person identify where God is at work in his or her life and how God is inviting him or her to respond to his work. More than anything, I am directing a person to listen to Christ's voice within—something I am incapable of doing if I haven't learned how to listen to the voice of the abiding Christ within me. Jesus said, "My sheep listen to my voice; I know them and they follow me" (John 10:27).

Active listening is perhaps one of the most important and sacred personal spiritual disciplines and ministries we can offer someone. It is the pathway to holy ground. This kind of attentiveness assists us in discerning the unfolding revelation of God's story—the story Jesus said is within us (Luke 17:21). But before we can coach another person to distinguish the Spirit's voice within, we must become proficient at recognizing and listening to Christ's voice within us.

EMBRACING SOLITUDE, BEFRIENDING SILENCE

For whatever reason, we often experience resistance when it comes to listening attentively to God's voice within our own hearts. This morning, as I spent time praying, I found myself distracted, drawn away from "being" with God and switching gears toward "doing" for God. It seemed that being held in silence by God was an uncomfortable and unnatural posture. My thoughts were pulled away as if by a strong magnet; my attention kept diverting to the periphery of life instead of attending to the center of Life within me.

I appreciate these words of Henri Nouwen: "Have you ever tried to spend a whole hour doing nothing but listening to the voice that dwells deep in your heart? . . . It is not easy to enter into the silence and reach beyond the many boisterous and demanding voices of our world and to discover there the small intimate voice saying: 'You are my Beloved Child, on you my favor rests.' Still, if we dare to embrace our solitude and befriend our silence, we will come to know that voice."

Embracing solitude and befriending silence are essential in order to locate the sound of his voice. Like both ears, working in tandem, honing the location of sound by its intensity and direction, time alone, in quiet, permits us to hear his voice. David described the path of listening this way: "Be still, and know that I am God!" (Psalm 46:10). "Let all that I am wait quietly before God" (Psalm 62:5). "I have calmed and quieted myself, like a weaned child who no longer cries for its mother's milk. Yes, like a weaned child is my soul within me" (Psalm 131:2). These verses describe entering into a place of rest, of being, where one becomes quiet enough to hear God's still, small voice of love. Do you know this place? Have you become proficient at entering solitude and becoming quiet in order to hear his whisper?

THE MINISTRY OF LISTENING

Once we begin to know this place of solitude and silence, once we begin to frequent it, our experience of hearing his voice within prepares us to listen to others with rapt attention, able to discern the Spirit's voice amidst their voice. I've learned in spiritual direction to attune myself to three elements: word choices, voice inflection and tears.

I remember when I began receiving spiritual direction, my director would often comment on a word I chose to express the deeper thoughts and feelings of my heart. At first, I thought it odd, as though my word choices were rather random and inconsequential. As I have studied and offered spiritual direction, however, I have learned that the words we choose often reveal something important. They serve as insight, often reflecting the way we perceive God, the world and ourselves.

A second element that is important to tune in to is a person's voice inflections. When you hear his or her speech become active and hurried or soft and pensive, pay attention to what he or she is saying. Changes in tone, pitch and rate are indications of emotions, sometimes pleasant and exciting and other times sad, painful or angry. When a person's voice reflects strong emotion, it's because his or her words come from a place of significance—a wound, a passion, a source of shame, anxiety or hope.

It is helpful to say, "I noticed when you talked about your experience that you sounded agitated and upset." If you lovingly hold up a mirror and help a person see how their feelings bleed through their speech, they often feel the freedom to admit, "Yes, I do feel fearful and anxious," or "No, I'm not afraid, but I do feel stressed."

Finally, pay attention to tears, no matter how subtle. The presence of tears is an indication that you are likely entering holy ground. It may be a place where God is hovering, eager to bring healing and freedom. It may be a place where this person needs the comfort of God's love and reassurance. It may be a dark closet that needs to be opened to God's light or something that needs to be affirmed, named into existence—a calling, a passion. Whatever the place, the entrance will often be marked by tears.

As an active listener, notice and acknowledge tears to the one to whom you are listening. Sometimes we overlook them, for fear of embarrassing the person. Yet it is far more awkward and hurtful for the person to feel missed—to feel as though we don't recognize and validate what he or she has divulged. Be an active listener and simply acknowledge, "I noticed your tears. Can you tell me what they mean?"

Real listening, active listening, requires undivided attention. When we truly listen, we offer others one of the most encouraging gifts they will ever receive. But listening always begins as a personal practice. It is the pathway to holy ground, discovered as we learn to recognize and attend to Christ's voice deep within us.

ACTIVELY LISTENING FOR THE VOICE WITHIN: A SPIRITUAL EXERCISE

You may not have an hour, as Nouwen alluded to, but spend fifteen minutes or more listening to the voice that dwells deep in your heart. Solitude and silence are the portals through which we enter this holy ground. As we quiet ourselves and learn to hear the Spirit's voice within, we will be more able to listen to others. Here are some suggestions:

- Begin by breathing deeply, calming yourself and being present to your own body.

- Sense or imagine the presence of God within you. Sometimes it helps to picture an image, like the one in John 15:5 where Jesus described himself as a vine and you as a branch, connected to the vine. Picture abiding in Jesus and him abiding in you.

- Be still and know that he is God (Psalm 46:10). Let all that you are wait quietly before God (Psalm 62:5). Calm and quiet yourself, like a weaned child who no longer cries for your mother's milk (Psalm 131:2).

- When a distracting thought comes, brush it aside with a mental broom. Don't scold yourself, just sweep it aside and return to being present to Jesus.

- Talk to Jesus directly. Use honest, heartfelt words to tell him what you are thinking or feeling.

- Listen with your heart. Listen for his voice within. Yearn to hear; lean into Christ as if straining forward with great attention, eager for him to speak. If nothing comes, don't worry. Stay with Jesus and rest with him.

2

SOUNDTRACK

by Brent

By day the LORD directs his love,
at night his song is with me—
a prayer to the God of my life.

PSALM 42:8 (NIV)

No matter how you route it, it's a long way from Indianapolis to Evansville. Especially if you go via Seymour. I had 225 miles, give or take a couple of tenths, to go. Road trip! Since I was traveling alone, I loaded up with music. I pulled out of Indianapolis to Carrie Newcomer's singing.

Then on the long and winding road from Seymour to Evansville (no, not the Beatles, despite this sentence's lead), God Help The Girl streamed out of the speaker. They have a sound that reminds me of '60s girl pop groups—not so much an imitation, though, as an homage. Next up was Jan Krist, an indy (as in independent, not Indianapolis) artist who composes singable melodies and thoughtful lyrics.

That was just on the way down. The highway back featured a whole 'nother musical set.

As I drove and listened, I thought about how much music makes up the soundtrack of my life. I like classical, jazz, bluegrass, roots and other styles. But I especially enjoy pop music. It's the music of my life on the road, heard from the tinny, tiny speakers in my first Volkswagen up through the full surround sound of today's twelve-speaker stereo array in my Toyota.

SPIRITUAL SOUNDTRACK

While cruising around southern Indiana musing on the music I listened to, I realized (not for the first time) that the tunes that truly speak to me often come from artists who possess a strong faith perspective. Besides Carrie and Jan (I have no idea about God Help The Girl—despite their name), that includes artists such as Over the Rhine, The Innocence Mission, Noel Paul Stookey, Pierce Pettis, Kate Campbell, Ed Kilbourne, Sufjan Stevens, Iron and Wine, and many more.

I am grateful for the care with which these musicians couch their cosmological consciousness and their spiritual sensibilities. They use nuance and whimsy. They don't preach. For the most part, regarding music, I do not need preaching. I need encouragement. I desire help for my pilgrim way. In many ways, these singers resemble the Old Testament psalmists, singing songs of the mysteriousness and majesty and wonder and frustration of this way of faith I try to tread.

That's why I picked the music I did for my trip. What kind of music do you need or want while on your pilgrim journey? What would you choose? Take a few minutes and write up a playlist for one of the following:

- for your next few hours

- as representative of your spiritual life

- for a particular difficult or joyful time of your life

What do your musical choices reveal to, or about, you? What do they say about how you practice your faith? Where does God show up in them?

TRAVELIN' TUNES

Singing and religious travels have long had a connection in my life. From the first time I climbed on the inexorably rusting old school bus with letters proclaiming Highland Avenue Friends Church and headed toward Mountain Lake Camp, songs and spiritual traveling were linked for me. In elementary school, we'd sing choruses like "Jesus Loves the Little Children" and rousing militaristic tunes like "I'm in the Lord's Army." As we, and the bus, grew older, our tunes changed to "Do Lord" and "Sing Hosanna." Later we added folk songs, show tunes, hymns, pop songs and hymns sung to pop tunes (did anybody from the late '60s and early '70s *not* sing "Amazing Grace" to the tune of "House of the Rising Sun"?). Leaving Young Life camp in Colorado, we sang "Rocky Mountain High." Not quite a hymn, but certainly a psalm to the week of spiritual growth that we'd experienced.

Of course, singing on pilgrimage is not something we started.

The Bible has a series of traveling songs—the Psalms of Ascents. The Israelites sang Psalms 120 through 134 as they made their way to Jerusalem for high holy days. Like our bus songs, they cover a wide range of subjects—from providence to joyfulness, harmony to service, blessings to obedience and much more.

These psalms are important for a couple of reasons. One is that we, like the Jews who sang them, are on a journey to God. These songs are about trying to be faithful to the Spirit's call while being faced with the realities of human life. Like them, we hear the voice of God call to us. We respond. But often our response falls short of what deep in our hearts we want it to be. These songs remind us travelers that we are not alone in our joys or sorrows, our faith or failings.

Second, these songs are not glorified, sanctified, Sunday-sanitized hymns. They are songs that deal with the realities of the human condition. Like many songs today, the psalms were written by real people with real frailties and faith. They express the agony and the ecstasy of what it means to be fully human—body, mind and soul. Our styles of living, transportation, work, roles in life and many other things have changed since these psalms were penned. But in the heart, where life matters most, people haven't changed at all. We, like the first psalm singers, want to be the best we can be for our family and friends and work and God. We want to love and be loved. We want to offer a shoulder to cry on or a joke to laugh at. And we want others to offer those things to us.

The Psalms of Ascents, these traveling songs, are more than a curiosity from a bygone era. They speak to us today.

Find your Bible and look at them now. See if there's one whose words sing to your spirit.

LISTENING TO GOD SONGS: A SPIRITUAL EXERCISE
You may be familiar with the spiritual exercise known as *lectio*

divina. *Lectio divina* is a contemplative way of reading and praying the Bible. It follows a rhythm (*lectio, meditatio, oratio* and *contemplatio*) that guides us into Scriptures and helps us connect with God.

While *lectio divina* is a deep spiritual experience, it is also grounded in our concerns, hopes, dreams and daily life as we interact with the Bible and seek guidance for the things facing us.

There's a variation on *lectio divina* called *audio divina*. I invite you to try it now. The first thing you need is a music source— whether full stereo or iPod with earbuds, doesn't matter. Next, choose a piece of music that is important to you and queue it up. Then find a place where you can be comfortable. Take some deep breaths. Fall into silence. After a few minutes of silence, play the music. As you play the music, move through these steps (you may want to put your music player on repeat so that you can listen to the piece over and over while doing *audio divina*):

- *Lectio*—listen for a word or musical phrase that particularly captures your soul's imagination.

- *Meditatio*—next spend prayerful time thinking about your word or phrase. How does it connect with your life? What feelings or images come to you? Spend time with these feelings or images and let them unwind in your imagination and heart.

- *Oratio*—ask how God is speaking to you in the current moment through the music. How are you experiencing God through the word or note? Make an offering to God of what you are discovering in your heart and imagination.

- *Contemplatio*—this is a time for resting in God. Slowly release the word or note and offer a prayer of gratitude for God's presence with you during this exercise.

Music enriches our lives, whether listening to road tunes or practicing *audio divina*. Music prompts us to prayer, praise, contemplation, action, meditation and obedience to the call of the Spirit. Let us give thanks for the soundtracks of our lives of faith. Let us sing a new song!

3

FOOTSTEPS

by Beth

Then the LORD God called to the man, "Where are you?"
He replied, "I heard you walking in the garden, so I hid.
I was afraid because I was naked."

GENESIS 3:9-10

One morning as I sat in bed, sipping my coffee and "coming to," I heard the sound of footsteps. It was David, walking from the kitchen toward the stairs to bring me a refill of coffee. I listened to his familiar, slippered feet padding up the stairway and felt a surge of gratefulness as I heard him come—a sense of anticipation, the gift of his goodness to me.

Footsteps—sometimes barely perceptible, other times sharp and distinctive—stir a host of feelings from joy and expectation to fear and dread. I think of hearing the early-morning shuffle of a toddler approaching my side of the bed to crawl in, or the rapid clipping of my grown daughter's high heels when she was late for work, or the footsteps of a stranger walking behind me in a dark parking lot—a scene moviemakers can't resist. In each of these examples, just hearing the sound of moving feet evokes strong feelings.

A friend of mine lived in the downstairs of a double that had hardwood floors. Every morning, the woman upstairs would get ready for work and put on shoes with heels. The closer it was to the time when she needed to leave, the faster and harder she would clomp. My friend said that simultaneously, as she got ready for work, a growing knot would form in her stomach from the sheer sound of the anxious, frantic footsteps upstairs. Subliminally, she began to feel as though she needed to hurry, that she was going to be late!

TELLING FOOTSTEPS

The way we respond when we hear a person's steps often depends on the sound they make. If the footsteps are hurried and pounding, we might suspect that something is wrong, that we are in trouble, or that he or she is in a hurry and we had better get out of the way. If the footsteps move quietly and stealthily, we might suspect someone is trying to sneak up on us. We might feel afraid and wary. If we hear casual footsteps, those of someone we have been anticipating—a spouse home from work or a teenager home for the evening—we feel relief or gladness.

From a young age, we even learn to differentiate footsteps—the telling footsteps of our parents, siblings, friends and teachers. Every person has a certain gait, a weight to their steps, a way they shuffle their feet that distinguishes them. I know which one of my kids has come home just by the way they enter our house, the pace at which they walk, the sound of their shoes. Our sense of hearing is remarkable to be able to decode a person's steps and know his or her identity.

Whose footsteps have you come to recognize without seeing them? How do you feel when you hear those steps? Have you ever wondered if you could hear the footsteps of God?

HEARING GOD'S FOOTSTEPS

One day, Adam and Eve heard footsteps in the Garden of Eden and recognized them as belonging to God.

When the cool evening breezes were blowing, the man and his wife heard the LORD God walking about in the garden. So they hid from the LORD God among the trees. Then the LORD God called to the man, "Where are you?"

He replied, "I heard you walking in the garden, so I hid. I was afraid because I was naked." (Genesis 3:8-10)

This scene took place during the evening, evidently a time when God frequented the garden to visit with his human friends. They immediately recognized the sound of his movement because it was familiar to them. But this time, instead of feeling a warm sense of anticipation, Adam and Eve felt dread. They had disobeyed clear instructions given to them by God. They had eaten fruit from the forbidden tree, felt shame and did what we typically do in that case—they hid from God.

This story provides an analogy of how we recognize God's figurative footsteps in our lives today. First, God frequented the garden during the evening when the cool breezes blew. He had a routine, a special place and time that he showed up to visit with Adam and Eve. Is it possible that God has a familiar and special place and time when he likes to come to visit with us?

Second, when God showed up, Adam and Eve recognized the sound of his footsteps. They distinguished them as God's before they ever heard his voice. That's because his movement was familiar to them. Is it possible that when God meets us in our garden, we can learn the sound of his footsteps and know that it is God?

Finally, Adam and Eve's response of hiding when they heard the sound of God's footsteps was the result of their own guilt and shame. They may have imagined God being disappointed or angry with them. After all, it was their own willful disregard of God's instructions that made Adam and Eve want to avoid his presence. Is it possible that we hide from God's visitations because of the way we feel toward ourselves or imagine God feeling toward us?

THE GARDEN OF WAITING

When I think of hearing God's footsteps in a familiar place, at familiar times in my life, I think of how often I have heard them in the "garden of waiting." The common theme in these recurring circumstances is my need to be patient and linger in the in-between until something is resolved. Consistently, in the process of simmering, I hear his footsteps and am brought to a place of surrender. I could list more than a dozen times when I have had to "cool my heels"—until a baby was born, my broken foot was healed, the house sold, the trial was over, I got the job or the offer to publish a book. One might suspect that this pattern addresses a character deficiency in patience and a stubborn commitment to self-rescue—and one would be right.

Most recently, I had an unexpected episode of waiting that involved an injury to my back. Having no previous issues with my back, this "garden" came out of nowhere. The pain became so acute that for two weeks, I lay flat on my back, knees tucked over a pillow, not moving. After visits to several doctors, I ultimately required back surgery to repair an extrusive disc.

During the time before and the recovery after, something about this "waiting pattern" felt very familiar—a place where I had been with God before. It was as though I heard his footsteps, padding around my waiting garden, looking for me. Because I had frequented this place, I knew that I could hide, resent my stay, fight what was going on or yield to it. After enough experience and recognition of how God had met me in this place previously, I entered the grace of surrender. This waiting garden, surprisingly, became a garden of intimate encounter with God—a place where he spoke to me and gave clarity about my passion and calling. When have you heard the footsteps of God? In what familiar garden has he invited you to come? In this next exercise, you will have the chance to identify memorable places where you have heard God's footsteps, where he has regularly met you. You will need a piece of blank paper and markers for this exercise.

THE FOOTSTEPS OF GOD: A SPIRITUAL EXERCISE

In this exercise, you will use a mind map or cluster to help you identify familiar places—gardens—where you have heard the footsteps of God and encountered him.

- Begin by drawing a circle or footprint in the center of the page. In the middle, write the words "Footsteps of God."

- Begin to brainstorm times and places during your life when you had a profound sense of God's presence and involvement in your life.

- When you think of one, use a different color marker and draw a circle adjacent to the center, connecting it to the center with a line, and write a few words to represent that time—like "back surgery." If you want to add details to describe this experience—words, Scripture, people or outcomes—write them in a cluster around the circle.

- Continue to do this, filling your paper with as many "gardens" as come to mind and feel significant.

- After you have finished, study your mind map and see if you recognize any familiar themes to your gardens: are there themes of waiting, loss, missed opportunities or risk-taking?

- How would you describe the footsteps of God in these gardens? What has become familiar about his presence and movement during these times?

- How have you responded to the sound of his footsteps? Have you ever hidden yourself? Why?

- What have you learned from returning to these gardens? How do you want to respond the next time you hear God's footsteps?

4

ALL THE NEWS

by Brent

I bring you good news that will cause great joy for all the people.

LUKE 2:10 (NIV)

I am inundated with news—expected and unexpected, from expected and unexpected sources. At 6:30 a.m. daily, I hear the news on television. I said "hear" because I'm not a morning person, so I usually "watch" the news with my eyes closed.

When I arrive at work, I hear news from my coworkers. Some tell me stories about what they did the night before. Others share updates of their plans for the day. Throughout our hours together, I hear news that, while often not as exciting as their stories of the night before, is important for how we manage the work God has given us.

I get news via telephone, instant messages and emails as well. One tells me about a friend's new grant for an arts project. Another informs me about another friend's possible job change. One asks for prayers for a loved one who's been stricken with cancer. Some of the news is good, some is sad, some is tragic. Of course, I like hearing the good news much more than I do the bad. Regardless, all the news I hear in a day connects me in God-ways with the wider communities of which I am a part—my friends, my coworkers, my city, my country, my world. By God-ways, I mean that many of the stories move me to pray—prayers of gratitude and prayers of supplication. Praying is something I always need to do more of.

ALL THE NEWS THAT'S FIT TO HEAR AND MORE

Not all the news that reaches our ears comes couched in language though. Sometimes it arrives via all the external noise that surrounds us. Sirens screaming down city streets outside our office windows. A cough from a coworker. The jackhammer thrum of construction.

Often these sounds are just background noise. Or worse, they're an annoyance. We're late for work and ready to go through the intersection when we hear a siren and stop and wait, then grumble when it turns a block away from us and we've missed the light. Or we're sitting quietly in church and a baby starts to cry just as the pastor begins her sermon.

Sometimes the sounds that surround us, but that we don't hear, could be blessings—the call of the robin in spring, a child's laugh of delight, the gurgle of a water fountain. We let them pass our ears by without noticing or being blessed by them. Sad.

There are few times in our lives when we are encased in complete silence. Even on a silent retreat we encounter sounds both natural and human-made. Ours is a noisy, noisy world—from chickadees chickadeeing to freeways humming even when they are miles away from where we are.

Take a moment and listen to the sounds around you. Pay attention to them in love. What sounds do you notice? What news are they bringing? Are they blessings or calls to prayer? Or both?

As you think about the sounds that compose the background soundtrack of your daily life, what words would you use to describe them? Are they sounds you should be paying attention to? Are they bringing news of others? Are they proclaiming God's story in a way that is different from how you normally hear it?

When listened to with attention and love, the everyday sounds of life may contain all the news of God that you can either use or bear.

PRAYING THE NEWS

There are days I'd like to take a news break. No, not a break for more news, but a break from any news. Much of the news sounds so bad that I'd just as soon not hear any more, thank you.

That's often how I feel as I hear the news unfold. But I am learning another way to approach this overabundance of bad news. And it's not new. For centuries, people have been praying intentionally about the events going on in the world around them. Throughout the ages, the faithful have found that praying for, and about, the news changes our perspective. Praying this way shifts the emphasis from our discomfort with tragedy to helping us hear it through the ears of the people it is happening to, and God's ears as well. It moves us from our role as compassionate (sometimes) but distant observers and puts us in the middle of the news. It shows us what it is like to be a person caught in the middle of an earthquake or bombing run—to hear the terror and fear. It asks us to imagine what it is like for God to hear his children's cries and see their tears. Praying the news invites us to unite with our sisters and brothers across the globe. It gives us a spiritual tool to use on their behalf.

That's why, for a number of years, the Carmelite sisters of Indianapolis hosted a website inviting visitors to join them in praying the news. Praying the news was nothing new to the sisters—they had been doing it for seventy-five years. Praying the news was the sisters' way of injecting prayer into the world's troubled situations.

Though they have since closed the website, it is a practice we can join them in using the tools from our own spiritual traditions, be they formal prayers, Scripture readings, litanies or prayers sprung fresh from the soul. The Carmelites explained that they prayed the news because "by making ourselves aware of the present moment of the universe, we awaken ourselves to our presence of God—and in our own way, participate in the healing, loving, and creative energy this process can spark."

One way to start praying the news is to begin by thinking about what news you have heard today. And then pray this prayer aloud:

Lord of compassion and wisdom,
How often do I exalt myself and look over you?
I look over the heads of my more humble brothers and
    sisters,
not seeing how they rely on you more than I do.
Help me to learn from them to make you the center of my
    life.
Give me the grace to see those around me who are
    brokenhearted.
Guide me in being with them in their sorrows.
I ask for the courage to help them with their needs
and be your hands and feet on this earth. Amen.

I suggest praying aloud because it helps us hear ourselves connecting what we have heard with supplication to God. This makes prayer a more sensory experience. Praying the news aloud moves us from wringing our hands and bemoaning "The horror, the horror," to actually doing something for God's sake.

PRAYING YOUR NEWS: A SPIRITUAL EXERCISE

We all have news that needs to be prayed for or about, even if we don't realize it. Think of all the sounds that have been a part of your life today.

- What's the news in what you've heard?
- Where is God in it?
- What is serious? sad? happy? dire?

How would you pray for your news? What spiritual tools would you use? Here are a few possibilities:

- written prayers
- spontaneous prayers
- Scripture readings
- prayer books

Whatever you use, take time to pray for your news—yourself.

5

RECURRING THEMES

by Beth

Haven't you heard? Don't you understand?
Are you deaf to the words of God—
the words he gave before the world began?

ISAIAH 40:21

A new world opened to me during my early teenage years—the world of classical music. I had begun playing the French horn the summer after fourth grade. I chose it because I fell in love with its sound. When I played, I found a way to express things inside me that I didn't know were there. My parents *never* made me practice—I practiced because I found joy in it. Soon after, I began studying with a professional musician from the local symphony orchestra who encouraged me to listen to classical music. My brother had a recording of Dvorak's *New World Symphony*—a glorious piece of music. It was the first symphony I tried. I would retreat to my attic bedroom, place the record on my stereo, turn it up as loud as I could and pretend that I was conducting the orchestra. (Okay, I'm not sure I've ever admitted that to anyone.) I became lost in the dark, rich, massive sounds—especially the French horns—and was transported to a new world.

One of the most striking features of Dvorak's *New World Symphony* is the recurring themes. Themes from the first movement are woven in and out of the three subsequent movements, subtly emerging from the densely woven fabric of the orchestration. Each time you hear the opening minor phrase recur, often by the brass section, you know you have reentered the new world—a world that takes courage to enter, but is expansive and filled with adventure.

RECURRING THEMES VERSUS TRENDS

When I think of recurring themes, I think of music like Dvorak's *New World Symphony*. However, recurring themes or repeating patterns show up not only in music but also in literature, art, math, nature and conversations. Often, when I hear the same ideas repeated in conversations, I take notice. For instance, I had lunch with two friends recently. In the course of the exchange, we talked about some things that we had been pondering. What I found interesting is that all three of us had been thinking and reading about many of the same things! I heard recurring themes.

Recurring themes differ from trends. They feel serendipitous; there is often a unique, uncanny quality about them. You hear them sounding from obscure, unexpected places—coming out of surprising mouths. Trends, however, are more like "group talk." We hear people energetically championing, for instance, "environmental consciousness," and then everybody gets on the "go green" bandwagon—an important wagon to be on! However, the problem with joining the chorus of a trendy theme is that it doesn't necessarily become our own value. We aren't motivated out of our own inculcated convictions but someone else's. I suspect that many trends begin as recurring unctions of the Spirit. Yet, at some point, they are compromised when the iteration simply becomes the next "cool" thing to talk and be about.

Many years ago, I began to hear a recurring theme, one that was in a dark, minor key. We were in a tough spot in our marriage. I was depressed and thought our struggles would never end. I found myself incessantly crying out to God, "Turn on the light!" During this difficult and painful landscape, I read a penetrating passage in Isaiah that began to haunt me—literally!

It started out, "Let the one who walks in the dark, who has no light, trust in the name of the LORD and rely on their God" (Isaiah 50:10 NIV). Walking in darkness was a perfect description of my life at the time. The passage went on to say, "But now, all you who light fires and provide yourselves with flaming torches . . . you will lie down in torment" (Isaiah 50:11 NIV). That scared me to death! Life felt hard and scary, but the last thing I wanted to do was light my own torch—to try and rescue myself—so that I could find my way out of the darkness!

Shortly after I read these verses, still sobered by their warning, I was talking to my friend Ann. She was amazed when I mentioned the passage and told me how her husband had recently read the same verses and had been thinking about them. He then shared this with a friend, who had *also* been reading and thinking about the same passage! Now that was weird.

A few weeks later, I opened a letter I received from some missionary friends. Plastered across the top of the letterhead was—you guessed it—Isaiah 50:10-11! The contents described my friend's journey into darkness and his reflections on this passage. Believe me, God had my attention!

Finally, a few months after that, I was at a women's conference where one of the speakers referred to "a letter she had received from missionary friends" and how they wrote about their experience of living through a dark, difficult time. Then *she read* Isaiah 50:10-11. I was astounded! Afterward, I talked with her and asked if, by chance, her friends were the same friends as mine. They were.

Have you ever experienced anything like this—a time when you kept hearing the same thing repeatedly? Perhaps the name of a book is mentioned by three different people in three different conversations. Or a person you haven't seen in a while comes to mind out of the blue, and the next day you hear from another friend that he or she is sick or has suffered a tragedy. Or you hear a sermon on the radio and then get to church to hear the pastor preach on the same passage of Scripture. Or someone shares a provocative quote, and the next day you see it on a card in the grocery store. One of the ways God speaks is through recurring themes. When we hear them, it is often a prompt to pay attention, pray for someone, think more deeply about something or watch for God's guidance.

Recurring themes are one of the ways we "hear" and recognize the voice of God in our lives. Suddenly it becomes clear to us that the repetition we are hearing isn't a result of happenstance, but the Spirit poking us, prodding us to pay attention. Through the uncanny conundrum of reverberating messages, God confirms to us that he has something to say. "Haven't you heard? Don't you understand? Are you deaf to the words of God—the words he gave before the world began?" (Isaiah 40:21).

What reiterating themes have you been hearing? What recurring tunes have arrested your notice? In this exercise, you will have the opportunity to reflect on the repeating patterns that have haunted you and what God might be saying through them.

RECURRING THEMES: A SPIRITUAL EXERCISE

For this exercise, choose a piece of music and listen to it. (If you don't have music handy on a CD or iPod, try Pandora Internet Radio on your phone or computer: www.pandora.com. Just type in an artist and away you go! It's free!)

- Listen for a recurring theme in the music. Notice how many times you hear it. Can you hum it?

- What do you notice about the theme and the way it is woven into the composition? How does the theme speak to you? How does it make you feel?

- What instruments play the theme? Which instrument is your favorite?

- As you listen to the theme, how would you describe the tone? If you could choose a color to match the theme, what color would it be?

- Now take some time to reflect on the last weeks and months of your life. Have you noticed any recurring themes? What are they? Take some time to write them in your journal.

- As you reflect on these recurring themes, how do they connect with you and your life right now? What aspect of your life do they speak to?

- What do you think God is saying through these repetitious refrains?

6

DINNER CONVERSATION

by Brent

When he was at the table with them, he took bread,
gave thanks, broke it and began to give it to them.

LUKE 24:30 (NIV)

Whatever would we have to talk about? That was my thought
one evening when I was going out to dinner with my boss, a board
of directors member and her husband. We composed a rather
eclectic group gathering at a restaurant in Washington, D.C. Despite the fact that about the only things we have in common are
our link to the Indianapolis Center for Congregations and that
each of us is a person of faith, things went very well. From the
time we climbed into the car until we reentered the hotel, the conversation was lively.

While we did not talk much about faith, it was the tie that
bound us together over dinner. Our conversation that night reminded me that while we are not all called to be the same type of
Christian, that's okay. As I pondered that, I also pondered the
words of seventeenth-century mystic Isaac Pennington:

> Oh, how sweet and pleasant it is to the truly spiritual eye to
> see the several sorts of believers, several forms of Christians
> in the school of Christ, every one learning their own lesson,
> performing their own peculiar service, and knowing, own-
> ing, and loving one another in their several places and differ-
> ent performances to their Master, to whom they are to give

an account, and not to quarrel with one another about their different practices. For this is the true ground of love and unity, not that such a man walks and does just as I do, but because I feel the same Spirit and life in him, and that he walks in his rank, in his own order, in his proper way and place of subjection to that: and this is far more pleasing to me than if he walked just in that track wherein I walk.

Dinner that night was just one example of how I am blessed to "see the several sorts of believers, several forms of Christians in the school of Christ" throughout my life.

MUTTS FOR THE HOUND OF HEAVEN
On the way back to the hotel, listening to the continuing conversations of Catholics, a Presbyterian and a Quaker, I realized that the next day's board meeting would add voices of other faith traditions. That reminded me of what a motley crew, religiously speaking, most of my friends are. One is a Lutheran who used to be Quaker. Then there's the Quaker who used to be Lutheran. And the United Methodist who was raised Baptist. There are Episcopalians, Nazarenes, nondenominational folk, and on and on.

Besides our many theological differences, we also live out our faith in different ways. Some of us believe in just war; others are pacifists. Some are prolife, others prochoice. We have all sorts of differences—politically, socially, culturally. Each difference is potentially divisive.

So why don't these differences tear us apart? Especially in these days when religious vitriol and mean-spiritedness seem to fill the airwaves?

Part of the answer lies in how we've chosen to listen to each other. As we've listened to each other's faith stories, we've quickly learned that every one of us feels called to follow God. Each of our spirits is hungry for the Divine.

Listening helps us understand why we live our calls out in different ways. Listening teaches us new ways of hearing Scripture, of praying, of talking about and relating to God. Listening helps us unplug our ears and open our minds to the idea that there is more than just one right way (mine!) to be a Christian. Hearing our friends' stories shows us that every one of us approaches faith with prayer, study and a deep desire for God.

By listening, my friends and I have come to respect the stories we've heard and the people who told them. This respect grows from faith in God and faith in the people who are our friends. Listening has taught me that all of them love God as much as I do. Even those who look or talk (religiously and ethnically) different from me.

Listening to each other with our physical and spiritual ears wide open helps my friends and me understand each other. In listening to each other this way, we have created spaces of theological hospitality where people feel comfortable sharing the deep experiences of their souls. They know they can share because they know that the hearts, as well as ears, of others are listening.

THEOLOGICAL HOSPITALITY

Finding a place for listening to each other is not as hard as we may think. Committee meetings are one such place. Most congregational committee meetings begin with a devotional thought. Instead of breezing through a hastily chosen biblical passage or perfunctory prayer, imagine the power and insight that folks could experience from having a different person open the meeting with a glimpse of their spiritual story. What fresh insights might we gain into life with God by hearing each other's spiritual journeys?

Another place for theologically hospitable listening is a Sunday morning adult class or a weeknight small group. Invite people to come prepared to share how they came to have the faith they have today. Or ask them to share their earliest spiritual ex-

periences. The ways of opening one another to our spiritual stories are unlimited.

You might get creative and have fun by using things like markers, PLAY-DOH, watercolors, paper, glue sticks and the like. Encourage people to use them to draw or make objects representing
something from their faith journey. Let the evening be a sort of
grown-up spiritual version of show-and-tell. After some initial
hesitation, I think you'll find folks having a great time with this
stuff that many of us adults never get to play with.

Though you may not think of it as such, by doing so, you're
actually inviting people to do more than share. You're helping
them make art in a special way for a special purpose. As Betsey
Beckman says, "Art-making is somehow all at once a journey, *a
communication,* a modality, a healing, and a prayer" (italics
mine). Such an activity welcomes people into sacred sharing
and prayer.

You can do this same faith exercise around the hot political and
social issues facing people of faith too. Ask participants where
they see God at work in their feelings about an issue. Preface the
time together by saying something like, "The only rule is that we
have to 'play nice.'" Give people time to express their feelings and
thoughts—from their faith perspective. How do their feelings
about these issues spring from their faith? Remind folks that the
purpose isn't to argue or dispute, but to hear how other faith-filled
people have come to the conclusions they have.

LISTENING FOR GOD: A SPIRITUAL EXERCISE

Such gatherings can be held salon-style at someone's home. A
home filled with love and life is a truly sacred space. And, since
God's people like to eat, why not host a meeting for eating and
listening? Inviting a small group of friends to meet together for
sharing snacks and spiritual journeys is a good way to listen to
each other and God.

As participants share, listen for

- beauty
- caring
- faith
- feeling in harmony with God
- gentleness
- goodness
- joy
- longsuffering
- love
- meekness
- peace
- persistence
- rightness

As you listen, you will find yourself hearing new ways of thinking about faith, ways that may complement and strengthen your own spiritual life. This is especially true for the times when you listen to someone whose way led them to a place that you would not, or did not, go.

A pad with chart paper might be helpful to record things like:

- What themes arose from the group as you shared?
- What words/phrases spoke to individuals?
- What words/phrases spoke to the group?
- What did you share?
- What differences were there?

I think you'll find that listening to each other with spiritual ears wide open leads us closer to each other—and to God.

Part Five

Smell

Art Reflection on Smelling

As you look at this chapter's illustration, take time to relax your body and mind. Breathe deeply. Think about the following questions slowly and gently as you look at this drawing. Savor each thought and each sensory experience that comes to you.

As you ponder the image of this man lifting a pot of coffee close to his nose to smell it, where are your eyes drawn?

Why do you suppose he draws the coffee pot closer to his nose? Describe how you think the coffee smells.

How would you define the expression on his face as he smells the coffee?

When are you most aware of the aroma of coffee? How do you respond to it?

If you were in his place, what other senses would be awakened? Describe them.

How does this picture inspire you? What does it make you want to do or smell?

An Aroma Pleasing (Leviticus 2:9) *is the title of this illustration. As you think of the enjoyment of aroma experienced by the man in the picture, what aromas please you? In what ways do you think you have been an aroma pleasing to God?*

Are there special scents at the beginning of your day that remind you of God and your life of faith?

What smells really get you going spiritually? Why?

1

INTRODUCTION

by Beth

So Jacob went over and kissed him.
And when Isaac caught the smell of his clothes, he was
finally convinced, and he blessed his son. He said, "Ah! The smell
of my son is like the smell of the outdoors, which the LORD has blessed!"

GENESIS 27:27

Of all the floral fragrances, gardenia is by far my favorite. I became infatuated with their scent on our wedding day. I don't recall being familiar with the smell of gardenias until my bouquet included several blossoms and effused a trail of the most luxurious perfume throughout the entire celebration. Sporadically, I would note a waft of their sweet aroma and drink it in. And even now, more than thirty years later, their distinctive smell evokes a vivid and beautiful memory; it resonates within me like an echo from the past, from one of the most important days of my life. I've grown so fond of this delicate fragrance that whenever David buys me perfume, he looks for something with a variation on the theme of gardenia.

SMELLING MEMORIES

Often the strongest memories of our past are indelibly imprinted into our memory bank through our senses, especially the sense of smell. Here's why: we use our olfactory sense all the time as we take in currents of air that pass through the nostrils and over the bony turbinates in our nasal passages to a "sheet" about the size of a small postage stamp, which contains five to six million olfactory receptors! There, smells are recognized because each odorant fits into a nerve cell kind of like a lock and key. The nerve cells then send signals along our olfactory nerve to the brain, where the odors are interpreted as "sweet-smelling gardenias" or "foul-smelling sneakers."

The reason we know the difference is the strong connection between our sense of smell and our memory. According to Dr. Rachel Herz, a psychologist, cognitive neuroscientist and recognized expert on the psychology of smell, our odor preferences are *learned*. An article discussing Dr. Herz's work claims that "we learn to like and dislike various odors based on the emotional associations we make upon initial encounter with them." That explains my romantic obsession with gardenias, and my warm association between snickerdoodles and my grandmother, and honeysuckle and my Aunt Edie. And it explains my repulsion to the smell of raw meat and the memory of my dad skinning and gutting animals in the garage after he went hunting.

Take a moment and think about the smells that are most notable to you. What do you associate with each? How do you react to each? Do you remember when you first smelled them?

Our sense of smell is integral to our memories. In fact, think about your most vivid childhood memories and see if many of them don't have an association with a smell: the barn at your grandfather's farm, fresh mown grass on a summer day, lightning bug "juice" on your hands and sparklers on the Fourth of July. Each is a very distinctive scent, rooted in a specific memory, even if we can't recall the precise day and time when we first noticed it.

The book of Genesis tells a story that illustrates the relationship between smell and memory. Jacob tricked his aging father, Isaac, into believing that he was his brother, Esau, so that he could steal his older brother's blessing. Jacob resorted to using smell as a convincing method of deception. Esau, a hunter and outdoorsmen, smelled of the hunt and the earth. When Jacob came in to see his father, he wore his brother's clothes, likely saturated with soil, sweat and the blood of wild game. "So Jacob went over and kissed him. And when Isaac caught the smell of his clothes, he was finally convinced, and he blessed his son. He said, 'Ah! The smell of my son is like the smell of the outdoors, which the LORD has blessed!'" (Genesis 27:27).

Isaac smelled and remembered. His eyes were failing, his legs weak, his taste buds dull. But his sense of smell was sharp and responsive. The moment he smelled Esau's clothes, the memory of his son and the association with the outdoors resonated within him. You can almost hear the "click"—the smell of earth and the recollection of Esau, a memory that brought extreme pleasure at its recalling. The scent was so convincing that Isaac was duped to believe that Jacob *was* Esau, and in turn gave him his blessing.

SMELL YOUR STORY

Smells have a way of helping us remember our stories—something important to do if we are to notice God's past involvement in our lives and participate with him in the present. They act as flags, tagging significant moments, events and people in our lives that have shaped who we are today. Of course, some memories of smells aren't pleasant, and perhaps are even painful and traumatic. In those cases, it's not uncommon for us to have to "resmell" the memory in order to experience healing from it.

A friend of mine lost her parents in a house fire when she was very young. Part of her healing journey has come through the "trigger" of smelling smoke. At first, when she had an encounter with smoke that reminded her of the house fire, it was very painful and frightening. The smell took her back to the memory as if she were living it again. With the skilled help of a caring therapist, she was able to recall and grieve the event and begin to heal from it.

Many of the smells from our past are positive and formative to our story. They remind us of significant and life-shaping people and experiences. We bring these images along with us, like a photo album that reminds us of where we've been or a thread that stitches our story together. In this next exercise, you will have the chance to name the smells that are most memorable to you over your lifetime and how they help you know your story. You will need a journal and, if it's helpful, a handful of favorite photos from your childhood until now.

SMELL YOUR STORY: A SPIRITUAL EXERCISE
Not everyone remembers his or her past with the same amount of detail. Recalling smells can help solicit memories with greater detail and allow you to revisit them and the important ways these people and experiences formed you as a person. So with journal in hand and, if helpful, a collection of six to eight of your favorite pictures from your past, take time to "smell your story" and remember the life-shaping activities of God in and through these people, places and events.

People:

- Begin this time of "smelling your story" by listing a few of the most formidable people in your life—those "iconic" figures who loom large in your memory. Look at pictures if that helps jog your memory.

- Choose one or two people who stand out to you as individuals who have influenced who you are today. Often their impact comes by simply being themselves and living their lives. As you identify a person or two, think back to what smells you associate with them: pipe tobacco, White Shoulders bath powder, motor oil, etc. What does that smell mean to you now? How did this person impact you?

Places:

- Now list a couple of places that were your favorite places to be or visit: homes, vacation spots, parks or places where you played. Look at pictures if that helps you remember.

- What did those places smell like? Describe the smells. What do the smells mean to you now? How did those places shape you?

Events:

- Finally, recall some of your favorite things you've done over your lifetime—events that have been formative to you or cherished experiences: picking apples, raking leaves in your yard, harvesting maple syrup, etc.

- What smells come to mind as you recall those experiences? Describe them. What do the smells mean to you? How have those events formed you?

2

SMELLS LIKE . . . WORSHIP

by Brent

The LORD smelled the pleasing aroma.

GENESIS 8:21 (NIV)

Quaker Meeting is not a smells-and-bells sort of worship experience. Friends have no rites, no rituals, no priests robed somberly or brightly, no scented smokes wafting from a censer. Yet there are smells that I associate with worship.

I realized that as I was settling into the Meetingroom where I had been worshiping daily while on a weeklong writing retreat. Like many Friends Meetingrooms, Pendle Hill's is a rectangular, light-filled space, lined with benches forming a square into the middle. I chose a backbench, as is my custom. Also, as is my custom, I settled in with my eyes closed. That's when the scents of worship came to me.

The first thing I smelled was wood warming as sunlight streamed into the room through the clear glass windows. The floor, the backs of benches and the windowsills released an aged wood scent that wrapped me in warmth and coziness. Then people smells came wafting by as the other worshipers drifted in. There was Doc's smoky scent—I had seen him puffing on his pipe in the parking lot prior to worship. Then came the fresh scent of Petra's perfume as she settled in the bench in front of me. Other smells soon filled the room, primarily the aromas of human bodies coming together in an enclosed space.

I breathed deeply and settled into worship. I wondered if this offering of worship would be considered a sweet-smelling sacrifice to the Lord. Surely it must, since the church is the body of Christ incarnate on earth. Bodies smell. Even (or especially?) the body of Christ. This mix of flesh, blood, spirit and mind creates a scent. Our lives smell—sometimes stinky, sometimes sweet. The sweet we don't mind; the stinky, on the other hand? "Now, can it be possible that in a handful of centuries the Christian character has fallen away from an imposing heroism that scorned even the stake, the cross, and the axe, to a poor little effeminacy that withers and wilts under an unsavoury smell?"

That's what Mark Twain wrote in response to a certain Rev. T. De Witt Talmage's op-ed piece. The good reverend had written, "I have a good Christian friend who, if he sat in the front pew in church, and a working man should enter the door at the other end, would smell him instantly. . . . If you are going to kill the church thus with bad smells, I will have nothing to do with this work of evangelization."

In worship, we mingle souls and bodies—and the scents that arise from them. Though it may not be a sweet-smelling sacrifice to us, or to Rev. T. De Witt Talmage, I imagine it all is to the Lord.

SMELLY SPIRITUALITY

Earlier that day, before worship, my new friend Bill told me about his father—a perfumer. Bill talked about how, as a kid, he watched his father create scents by mixing and matching various fragrances to develop something pleasing to the nose. I thought of the perfume that we were creating as we brought our various fragrances to worship—to God.

The idea that the human and divine experiences of scent and the sacred intertwine is not new. The Hebrew Testament contains many exhortations to make sweet-smelling sacrifices to the Lord. And the apostle Paul tells us that "we are to God the pleasing aroma of Christ" (2 Corinthians 2:15 NIV).

The early church knew that scent was an important part of experiencing God. Unlike many churches today, the early Christians understood that since the church was the body of Christ, then our physical senses would be as involved in experiencing God's kingdom as our spiritual senses. That's very similar to what writer Mary Gordon says: "The incarnate God is a potent embodiment of what I think of as the truth about the human lot: that we are mixed, flesh, blood, spirit, mind—and that the holy is inseparable, not only from matter, but from the narrative of our lives."

As liturgies and rites evolved, church leaders used scents to teach. They assigned meanings to different smells—good scents were signs of saintliness, and bad smells indicated sinfulness. Early Christians believed that pleasant scents were an indication of God's presence with the worshiper. Susan Harvey writes that "knowledge of God was instilled in the believer who inhaled the scent of worship." That the Holy Spirit had touched a person was obvious by the way they smelled. They literally were the aroma of Christ (or not!) to those who encountered them.

The use of heavily scented holy oil was also a primary part of initiation into the Christian community. One of these holy oils, still used today by some rites, has forty-seven various fragrances blended into the oil. Indeed, the use of scent is not uncommon among Orthodox, Anglican and Catholic congregations today. These traditions use the sense of smell to enlighten the minds and souls of those who worship. The aromas help bring them, body and soul, into communion with Christ. The scents in such congregations come chiefly through the holy oil and incense. But it's also common to decorate a church's interior with aromatic flowers and herbs. When Orthodox rites celebrate Pentecost, for example, their temples are often filled with fresh-cut flowers and foliage. Many times those gathered for worship stand clasping flowers, buds or blossoms during worship.

Many of us nonliturgical types, though, are completely unused to fragrance as a part of worship, unless it is Sister Edna's liberally applied Shalimar.

Pretend that you are one of the leaders of the early church—except that the early church is getting started today! As you assemble rites and rituals and ways to teach the faith, what scents would you use? Or would you have any intentional scents at all? What scents would you use to represent worship to you? Consider scents for the following:

- for God the Father
- for Jesus
- for the Holy Spirit
- for the Bible

SCENTS-ING THE SPIRIT: A SPIRITUAL EXERCISE

We take a breath between 14,000 and 17,000 times each day. Every time we breathe in, we inhale the aromas of the world around us. Some of these smells are delightful. Some are less so—perhaps like the disdained body odor of Rev. T. De Witt Talmage's nineteenth-century working man. Regardless, these smells connect us to all of creation and to God, the creator of it all.

Take a few minutes and think of the place where you most often sense God's presence. This may be where you worship on Sunday mornings. Or it may be a park where you go for walks, a corner of your living room or some other place. Close your eyes and relax. Think back to the most recent time when you felt God close there. Then consider the following questions:

- What did that place smell like then?

- What scents come to your mind?

- Are they scents of people? objects? food?

- How do those scents contribute to your sense of divine presence?

- Do they help connect you to God when you smell them out of context, at places or times where or when you don't expect to smell them?

- Do these things speak to you of God and faith? Or not?

Think back on various churches or holy places you've visited and see if you can recall what they smelled like. Did they smell like what you imagined? Why or why not?

You can also use your sense of smell as a prayer device—to offer prayers for what the smells evoke. Perhaps

- gratitude for the fresh fragrance of newly mown grass

- concern for the homeless woman who obviously has not been able to bathe for a while

- thanksgiving for the scent of food and the person preparing it as you open the door at the end of a long day

- care for the earth as you breathe in a noseful of smog

What scents bespeak the holy for you? Take a deep breath now—through both your nose and your soul. What do you smell—literally or soulfully—that reminds you of God and worship? Hold that scent in your spirit as you move through the day. Allow it to keep your soul in a place of worship even as you go about the busy clamorings of life. Let it usher you into God's presence in the deepest part of you. Breathe deeply the goodness, the wonder, the worship of God.

3

HOSPITALS

by Beth

Are any of you sick? You should call for the elders of the church to come and pray over you, anointing you with oil in the name of the Lord. Such a prayer offered in faith will heal the sick, and the Lord will make you well.

JAMES 5:14-15

I can still recall walking down the hallway of the surgical floor; the permeating mix of antiseptic and adhesive smells reminded me of Band-Aids. It was a familiar odor, yet altogether distinctive. We were there to pray with a close friend who was undergoing a serious surgery. At the age of thirty, an athlete her entire life, she was having an operation to reconstruct her hip joint. The surgical procedure lasted five hours. It took her two months of recovery and therapy before she could even put weight on her hip. I visited the hospital twice in two days, and both times I noticed the hospital "tang."

At the very same time, in a hospital only a few miles from my friend, two of my daughters stood vigil with another almost thirty-year-old woman. This one was losing her grip on this life. She'd had breast cancer for almost five years and had developed life-threatening complications over the weekend. Her family and close friends gathered to form a circle of support, their aching hearts clasped together in grief, stubbornly clinging, unwilling to give up the fight with her.

My varied portfolio of hospital memories includes a few of my own: a tonsillectomy at seventeen, four babies in five years and a recent back surgery. It also holds recollections of visiting a host of family, friends and parishioners. I recall as a teenager visiting my mom in the hospital during a stay for clinical depression—a difficult memory. A second picture also comes to mind: sitting in the devastating silence of my dad's hospital room after we found out that he had terminal cancer with only a year or so to live. One final image in the album stands out as well: sitting at the bedside and praying over the motionless body of another woman in her thirties who was on life support, the culminating effect of anorexia. She never awoke.

I have visited and prayed for people having minor and major surgeries and illnesses, some who recovered and some who didn't. No matter what the occasion, every time I enter a hospital, I've been seized by the copious smells that are symbolic to me of suffering *and* of the miracle of healing.

Overall, I experience a hospital as a sacred shelter, a place where the sick are gently held so that others who know how to care for them can do so. I am profoundly grateful for hospitals, for all the healing potential we have at our disposal in this country—at least many of us. When I smell "hospital," I see a hallowed place. It is a place where, as a pastor, I have offered prayer for healing and sometimes walked with the languishing to the edge of the valley of death and eternity with God. I have no trouble imagining the Spirit hovering amidst the blend of medicinal potions, ministering through the prayers of those who bleed them, doing the work of curing and in some cases extricating—extricating spirits from their earthly bodies, releasing them to their eternal home.

However, I realize that some people can't stomach the odor of hospitals—it brings back bad memories or incites overwhelming fears. Many feel queasy when they enter a hospital and encounter the cocktail of scents. I've heard of people who faint or get sick when they inhale potent hospital smells.

ANOINTING OIL AND HEALING PRAYER

One of the unique features of hospital smell is the fact that it isn't isolated to one place or thing. Often when you smell an odor, it's restricted—a spoiled container of cottage cheese or a dirty diaper. But in a hospital, the sterile whiff permeates every nook and cranny. It's invisible and everywhere. As such, the smell of a hospital can stir us, if we allow it, to engage with the omnipresent Healer, the One who lingers at each bedside of those we love and for whom we are called to pray.

During biblical times, healing ministry didn't happen in an institution but in a home. If there was an overriding smell to this first-century hospital, it was likely the aroma of olive oil mingled with spices. Oil was used medicinally to clean wounds as well as anoint the sick and dying and pray for them. When Jesus commissioned his disciples for ministry, he must have modeled anointing with oil and healing prayer: "So the disciples went out, telling everyone they met to repent of their sins and turn to God. And they cast out many demons and healed many sick people, anointing them with olive oil" (Mark 6:12-13).

Practicing medicine is a more sophisticated science today. However, our approach to doctoring may sadly overlook the holy and divine intervention so often needed—an inference that the aromatic fragrance of oil likely conjured in the hearts and minds of early believers. How might we recapture the scent of God's healing power and presence amidst the mingled smells of a hospital? Is there a way to enter the ethereal world where Spirit and medicine conduct their curative work *together*?

RECLAIMING AN ANCIENT PRACTICE: A SPIRITUAL EXERCISE

God spoke through the prophet Jeremiah with grave disappointment at his followers' apathy toward the ministry of healing and prayer: "They dress the wound of my people as though it were not serious. 'Peace, peace,' they say, when there is no peace. . . . Is there no balm in Gilead? Is there no physician there? Why then is there no healing for the wound of my people?" (Jeremiah 8:11, 22 NIV).

Could it be that God is asking the same question of us today?

Perhaps it is time to reclaim an ancient practice. Rather than recoil from the unpleasant smell of hospitals and bedsides, what if we introduced a different fragrance, the perfume of anointing oil and healing prayer? (In some Christian traditions, this is not a new or neglected ministry but practiced often and in faith.) In this exercise, you can purchase oil from a local religious gift store or online, or you can secure a few simple ingredients to make your own fragrant oil to use for healing and prayer. (By the way, making the oil can be a wonderful sensory experience that adds much to the exercise.)

Cold-Infused Healing Oil

1. Gather or purchase some fragrant herbs or flowers like lavender, rosemary or mint. You will need enough to fill a small jar. Lay the herbs or flowers in a single layer on a cookie sheet lined with paper towels. Set it in a dark, cool place for a few days until the herbs or flowers are completely dried out. (Though fresh herbs are best, you can skip this step and use dried ones as well.)

2. Tear or crush the herbs and then lightly pack them into a clean, sterilized glass jar. For fresh herbs, fill the jar to the top. For dried herbs, fill the jar about one-third full.

3. Pour a high-quality, cold-pressed virgin olive oil over the herbs, leaving two inches of room at the top.

4. Stir lightly to get rid of any air bubbles.

5. Cap the jar and label it. Store it in a cool, dark place (out of direct sunlight) for two to six weeks at the most.

6. After six weeks, strain out the herbs through cheesecloth, twice if you have to, then pour the oil into a clean, sterile bottle or jar.

After you have made your oil or purchased it, begin using it by praying for yourself.

- Open the lid or cap of oil and breathe in the fragrance. Let it infuse your palate with its perfumed aroma. Sit for several minutes and enjoy the smell.

- Take a small amount of oil on your fingertip. Place a dab of oil on your forehead, wrists, heart or any place where you need healing. If you like, make the sign of the cross, anointing your body in the name of the Father, Son and Holy Spirit.

- Ask God to heal you from the inside out. Sit for a time, smelling the fragrant oil and opening yourself to God's healing.

- Ask God if there is anyone he wants you to pray for who needs healing. If someone comes to mind, consider asking him or her if you might come and pray.

- Follow the practice of early Christians: "Are any of you sick? You should call for the elders of the church to come and pray over you, anointing you with oil in the name of the Lord. Such a prayer offered in faith will heal the sick, and the Lord will make you well" (James 5:14-15).

4

SEA SALT AND MIDWEST MULBERRIES

by Brent

In simple trust like theirs who heard
Beside the Syrian sea
The gracious calling of the Lord,
Let us, like them, without a word
Rise up and follow Thee

JOHN GREENLEAF WHITTIER

This place smells different from my Indiana. The heat and humidity are about the same in Indiana as here today, but their scents are decidedly different. While writing this I am relaxing at one of my favorite places, Bald Head Island, North Carolina. I started coming here years ago, and the island has not lost its charm. Bald Head is a quiet island south of Wilmington where no internal combustion vehicles are allowed. As I sit in silence and type, the sun is sinking and the ocean shines silver in the waning sunlight. The waves are up. The smell of salt fills the air.

The salty smell of the sea reminds me of the vastness of God's creation. That smell reminds me, too, that the same God who created the Midwest with its deep dirt, woods and glens, rivers and streams, and masses of wildflowers also made this place with its unique beauty of sand, sea, sun, horizon, maritime woods and marshes.

I admit to having seen little of this world. Yet the sights and smells of each place I visit show me dimensions of God that I could not have apprehended anywhere else. "All the way to heaven is heaven," said Catherine of Sienna. My travels show me that Catherine was right.

Bald Head Island is important to me, and not just because I could be its namesake given my hairline (or lack of one). It has become a sacred space in my life, a place of wonderful family gatherings and deep spiritual experiences. All tinged with the scent of sea salt in the air. When I smell that salt air, I know I am coming to a place of relaxation and worship, both in communion with other Christians at the Bald Head Island Chapel and privately as I spend time walking on the beach or in the maritime forest.

When I'm riding the ferry to and from the island, I watch the myriad fishing boats. Seeing them calls to mind Jesus and the disciples out in tiny boats on the Sea of Galilee. Thinking about that makes those stories more alive to me, populated as they are with breathing human beings sniffing in scents as they rocked out on the waves.

SCENTS-ING SCRIPTURE

While the scent of sea salt did not fill their noses (the Sea of Galilee was a freshwater lake), the disciples still would have experienced the roll and rock of boats out in deep water, the smell of freshly caught fish, and the aroma of hard-working bodies baking under the sun. On one of my ferry trips, I found myself wondering what smells they experienced as they lived out one of my favorite stories.

One day as Jesus was standing by the Lake of Gennesaret, the people were crowding around him and listening to the word of God. He saw at the water's edge two boats, left there by the fishermen, who were washing their nets. He got into one of the boats, the one belonging to Simon, and asked him to put out a little from shore. Then he sat down and taught the people from the boat.

When he had finished speaking, he said to Simon, "Put out into deep water, and let down the nets for a catch."

Simon answered, "Master, we've worked hard all night and haven't caught anything. But because you say so, I will let down the nets."

When they had done so, they caught such a large number of fish that their nets began to break. So they signaled their partners in the other boat to come and help them, and they came and filled both boats so full that they began to sink.

When Simon Peter saw this, he fell at Jesus' knees and said, "Go away from me, Lord; I am a sinful man!" For he and all his companions were astonished at the catch of fish they had taken, and so were James and John, the sons of Zebedee, Simon's partners.

Then Jesus said to Simon, "Don't be afraid; from now on you will fish for people." So they pulled their boats up on shore, left everything and followed him. (Luke 5:1-11 NIV)

When I close my eyes and imagine that story as if I were there, I breathe in the scents of the lake water, wet wooden boats, dripping nets, fishermen who had worked all night and the crowd of people pressing against Jesus, hoping to hear him.

What is your favorite Bible story? Take a few moments to recall it now. What smells do you associate with it, even if you've never quite thought of smelling it before?

- What is the smell of the air?
- The scenery where it is taking place?
- The people?
- Are there animals present?
- What about trees or flowers?
- Is food cooking?

Using your sense of smell is a way of bringing stories to life in a fresh way.

SMELLS LIKE HOME

Another thing I thought about as I made my way from the mainland was how those seaside fishermen's everyday lives were filled with smells. Just like mine. I experience office smells, city smells, home smells. I wondered what aromas told them they were home:

- Wet nets drying in the sun?
- The smells of onions, garlic, cumin, coriander, mint, dill and mustard as dinner cooked?
- The scent of their families?
- The scent of the synagogue?

All of these, while familiar as certain scents are in our lives, had to feel like God's blessing when life was good. They were the smells of their special place. As the great theologian Dorothy Gale said, "There's no place like home." Their home was Palestine. My home, in a way that is very spiritual and definable in no small part because of its smell, is the lower Midwest.

In the same way that Saint Paul tells us that we are to be "rooted and grounded" in Christ's love so that we "might be filled with all the fulness of God" (Ephesians 3:17-19 KJV), I find that I am rooted and grounded in the Midwestern soil. This particular place with its certain smells speaks to my soul with its lush greenness, multiplicity of flowers and grasses, tall trees, manageable vistas and scents, corn fields in humid night air, freshly mown grass, crisp snow blowing cold from the west, smoky autumn bonfires, muddy creek water, freshly turned soil in springtime and even the reek of over-ripened berries falling from the myriad mulberry trees around my house.

The Midwest is my home. This is my vision of heaven, both here on earth and in eternity. Good-hearted women and men rejoicing (though subtly) in the blessings of God, land abundant and fertile, life a wee bit slower when I allow it to be, and God feeling near.

I am rooted and grounded in this place.

A SENSE OF SCENT: A SPIRITUAL EXERCISE

The smells I experience daily allow me to experience the extravagantly creative side of God—the landscapes and seascapes, the scents and sights, the sounds and the feel of the planet we call home. All of this created for no other reason, as far as I can tell or read in Scripture, than the pure pleasure of the creative act and for our enjoyment and sustenance, both physical and spiritual.

What are the everyday smells that root and ground you to your place? It may not be the place that you reside in now, though most likely it is.

- How do the smells of "home" bless you?
- What do they tell you about God when you think about them as blessings?
- In what way do these smells tell you that you're home?
- What emotions do they bring to mind?

The scents of my existence connect me with people of faith throughout the ages, from fishermen who must have smelled similar scents to those I smell while rocking my way out across the Cape Fear River to early abolitionist pioneers who smelled the Midwest essence on their way to a land free to all, including slaves. When I smell salt in the air, mulberries rotting on the ground and countless other aromas that accompany me through life, I give thanks for them.

What scents swell your soul with gratitude? Make a quick list of them now—both what they are and why they cause you to feel grateful.

As you look them over, take time to pray for the people, places and other things that they bring to mind. Give God thanks for them and lift them up as a blessing from and to God. Use the scents of your life as a prayer tool to remind you via your nose to pray for those people and things they bring to mind.

In that way you may move through your day with a new sense of holy "scents-ibility."

5

ORGANIC SWEAT

by Beth

But blessed are those who trust in the LORD
and have made the LORD their hope and confidence.
They are like trees planted along a riverbank,
with roots that reach deep into the water.
Such trees are not bothered by the heat.

JEREMIAH 17:7-8

Over the summer, David and I went for an early morning walk during a period of record-breaking temperatures and oppressive humidity that swept across large areas of the country. Even though it was before 8 a.m., the temperature was in the 90s with 90 percent humidity. As we slogged along our usual loop, I became aware of a familiar, sweet, musky smell in the air. I asked David how he would describe it. About that time, we caught a strong whiff of "bio-steam" radiating from the plants, trees and ground, and then he named it—organic sweat. Yes. Very apropos.

It's the smell of wet, earthy, marshy, decomposing plant matter. It's heavy in the air, hanging like a damp sheet on a line, unable to dry. The official name is *transpiration*—plant sweat that is the result of moisture being drawn up through the roots all the way to the leaves where the moisture evaporates. (A large oak tree can transpire forty thousand gallons of water in a year!) The smell reminded me of humus—a compost of decayed plants and animal excrement that gardeners add to enrich soil. (Not to be confused with hummus—a wonderful, Middle Eastern dish made from chickpeas and tahini.) As we smelled organic sweat, it had this intense quality—natural but not altogether pleasant.

Transpiration is the heaviest when the temperature outside is extremely hot. Plants and trees work extra hard to draw moisture from the soil to hydrate and cool themselves, just like humans. Our bodies have a built-in cooling system that excretes moisture to lower our body temperature. The moisture we produce is a combination of oily, glandular, sweaty smells—natural but not altogether pleasant. Among both vegetation and humanity, sweat helps keep us alive, keep us from burning up.

A whole industry exists for the elimination of bodily, human smells and sweat. Body washes, soaps, deodorants, body sprays and colognes are designed to cover up our natural scent and eliminate sweat. These products are not always successful, but they do a decent job of masking the stinky smell and sticky sensation of b.o.—something we tend to be self-conscious of and uncomfortable with. Yet what is more natural than organic or human sweat? It serves an important purpose in living things by drawing moisture from our "roots," increasing our circulation, hydrating and cooling us so that we don't expire in oppressive heat.

WHEN LIFE MAKES US SWEAT

That's the picture Jeremiah painted as he compared people of faith to a tree: "But blessed are those who trust in the LORD and have made the LORD their hope and confidence. They are like trees planted along a riverbank, with roots that reach deep into the water. Such trees are not bothered by the heat" (Jeremiah 17:7-8). Such trees (or people, that is) aren't bothered by the heat. Why? Because they have the ability to draw from their spiritual roots and cool themselves down.

Sometimes life circumstances heat up as though smothering us in a wet, sticky blanket of problems, expectations and challenges. The temperature escalates; we feel like we're living inside a pressure cooker. Troubles come our way, one after another, and we can respond either as the tree Jeremiah described or as the plant that Jesus talked about, which "soon wilted under the hot sun, and since it didn't have deep roots, it died" (Mark 4:6). Rooting and sweating—just like organic matter—are what we do to survive during times of intense stress.

When David and I walked along, taking in the atmosphere of humus-like smells that early summer morning, it was as though we could feel the plants and trees being very still, taking deep drinks from their roots, exhaling moist air and cooling themselves. In the following exercise, you will discover a helpful form of praying, using your sense of smell and breathing. It will teach you how to root yourself in Christ and cool down when life becomes overwhelming and intense.

KEEPING OUR COOL: A SPIRITUAL EXERCISE

Breathing is typically an unconscious act and essential to our sense of smell. In order to smell, we have to breathe in through our nose, drawing in the odors and scents around us in order to identify and, in some cases, enjoy them. Many smells are subtle and go unnoticed because we don't allow them to register in our conscious minds. As we slow down and become more aware of our breathing and smelling, we begin to notice scents, calm down and become present to God.

- Begin by breathing slowly through your nose, paying attention to any smells that linger around you: food, candles, flowers, perfumes, leather furniture or outdoor smells.

- Continue breathing through your nose and specifically pay attention to how you smell. Can you smell your skin? your clothes? your own scent? your own sweat?

- Keep noticing smells as you establish a comfortable rhythm of breathing and become relaxed and calm.

- Take a long, deep breath as you inhale. Let a long, deep breath out as you exhale.

- For several minutes, continue to slowly take breath in and exhale breath out. As you do, imagine inhaling and smelling the peace of God as you exhale your burdens and worries.

- What does God's peace smell like to you? Imagine the fragrance of his peace permeating your soul.

- Take a few minutes and write in your journal a description of the fragrance of God's peace.

6

WAKE UP AND
SMELL THE COMMUNION

by Brent

I'm on my second cup of coffee and I still can't face the day.

GORDON LIGHTFOOT

I should be more careful about saying yes. But I am a slow learner. So when my friend Katie called and asked if I would pick her up at the airport, I said yes—without first checking the details. After I agreed, she then told me that her plane was due in around 11:30 p.m. This is well after my usual bedtime of 10 p.m.—which is also known as Quaker midnight.

But a promise to a friend is a promise. So even though Katie texted me around 10:30 saying they were just getting ready to take off from Atlanta, I stayed awake, ready to do my friendly duty. I tracked her flight on the Internet, and when my flight-tracking software said her plane had landed, I headed for the airport.

I forgot that we'd have to wait on her luggage.

So it was past 12:30 a.m. before we wandered into the house.

I went straight to bed, telling Katie to sleep in if she felt like it.

"Will you sleep in?" she asked.

"Probably not," I replied.

Sure enough, right at the crack of 6:30, as usual, I was awake. Well, sort of. My body brought my mind out of slumber into an awareness that it was time to get up, even though my brain didn't want to. Not at all. But I could not get back to sleep. Happily, I was eased into the new day by the smell of coffee brewing. Nancy, who always beats me up (hmm, that doesn't sound quite right!), had been up for an hour. The aroma of the fresh coffee she brewed filled the air. It made me feel almost alive.

Almost.

Oh, in case you were wondering, Katie slept in. Soundly, I hear.

CAFFEINATED COMMUNION

Later that morning, after I had dragged myself into the office, I smelled fresh coffee again. A coworker had made his way into the office, turned on his computer and brewed a fresh pot of coffee. He does that every morning. I was grateful because the smell perked me up again. And I began acting almost awake and started conversing with people. Often I begin to think of coffee as a sort of communion when I smell that heavenly aroma.

Coffee is a form of communion in many places and for many people—if by communion we mean communing with other people as well as God. I've had many a deep conversation about life and God with a friend over coffee at the local brewhouse. And there have been a number of times we officemates have gathered while pouring Coffee-mate into our cups and recapping our weekend's activities. And I can't count the many cups of joe I have enjoyed in between Meeting for Worship and Firstday (Sunday) School.

While I often have enjoyed communion with my friends and family over coffee, I also maintain that I have had communion with God in those moments as well. Both in the God whose Spirit lives in us, whether we're at church or in the kitchen at work, and through the goodness that comes from God's gift of coffee to us. All good things, including coffee, come from God. They are given for our pleasure and are a means of drawing us closer to God.

Perhaps you have never thought of communion that way, as something outside of a sacred ritual performed in a congregational setting. Take a few minutes and think about what scents you associate with communion—either as part of the holy rituals of your faith tradition or as daily as brewing coffee.

I DON'T SMELL A THING

The aroma of brewing coffee (fair trade, of course) often makes me think about the role of smell in my life. I can't imagine not being able to smell. Yet one of the most important people in my life is unable to sense scent. My dad lost his ability to smell as a result of a traumatic work accident that almost took his life. He doesn't mention much anymore that he can't smell. I often forget that scents have no scent to him. I may wrinkle up my nose at some unpleasant odor and ask, "What's that stink?" Dad just arches his eyebrows at me and shrugs, as if to say, "How would I know, doofus? Forgotten I can't smell?"

How do you think that not being able to smell would affect how you experience communion, either with those you love or with God?

Scents are revelations of God. We may not often think of them that way, but at certain sublime moments in our lives, when deep spiritual moments merge with physical senses, smells become containers of divine revelation. And these revelations are believable and incredibly moving precisely because they are happening in the midst of everyday experience without either denying its ordinariness or its sacredness. Sadly, using our sense of smell, or any of our other physical senses, is something about which few teachers or preachers speak today. It is as if we are to pick up our spirits only, not our bodies, to follow Jesus. But without bodies that touch, hear, smell, see and taste, it is impossible to pick up our crosses, as Jesus calls us to do.

Yes, the scent of coffee as communion may seem a bit of a stretch (especially to high church readers), but it serves as a useful metaphor. And, as writer and professor Edward Lueders says, "The way to know God has always been by way of metaphor."

What smells, metaphorically or in reality, help you know God? What spiritual (and other) scents would you miss if you were no longer able to sense them? How would your experience of God—either literally or metaphorically—be poorer if you could not smell?

SCENTS OF THE SPIRIT: A SPIRITUAL EXERCISE

Take a breath now. A deep one. What do you smell? Try it again and pay attention in love to the scents you're inhaling. True spiritual smelling involves all of the following:

- receiving the scents that are there
- understanding that what we're smelling can be a gift
- seeing that scents-ing like this is an opportunity for soulful contemplation
- realizing that life is not just about us; it is also about what we are smelling

Smelling this way helps us sense (physically and spiritually) in fresh ways the interconnectedness we have with what we smell and God. Drawing in aroma this way opens us to an attitude of awe.

Smelling with attention and love and spiritual intent is about uncovering revelation in the midst of mystery. Holding our noses, whether at stinky people or other unpleasant aromas, closes us off from each other and God. Pat Koehler reminds us that "we are called to openness, and sin is closing off ourselves from mystery. Closing ourselves to mystery is closing ourselves to God." Holding our noses closes us off to God.

So open wide and breathe deep. Inhale the scents of life deep into your lungs and soul. Where is communion with God and others in what you're taking in?

Does what you're smelling right now tell you anything about what your soul needs?

- Communion?
- Healing?
- A word from God?
- A fresh breath of the Spirit?

Use your sense of smell as a way of inhaling God's energy and goodness deep into your body and Spirit.

Do you want to come closer to God? Just follow your nose.

CONCLUSION

Rhythms That Ground Us

Our senses are extraordinary conduits through which we experience daily doses of God's wonder. Each one is a receptor of God's presence emanating from all with which we come in contact. As you have read this book, have you begun to live more in touch with your physical senses? Have you been awakened—your whole brain, all five senses and body—to experience more of God?

We have described a way of living—*a lifestyle*—throughout these chapters. A life as a spiritual sensate can't be confined to a devotional hour set aside each day. To be sensuous Christians, we must live globally, openly and responsively to the world around us. In doing so, we find the Divine within that world inviting, inspiring, teaching, speaking and revealing fresh aspects of God's self.

Living this way involves a substantial shift for most of us. Usually, we zoom through our days, our minds in high gear, zipping along with such force and thoughtlessness that little of God's presence and revelation registers to us. So at first, it may seem daunting to contemplate making such a radical lifestyle change. It's hard to imagine consistently paying attention in love to God's presence in the world around us. It can be done, however, by making small adjustments and taking small steps over time.

OUR HUNGER FOR BEAUTY

We hunger for beauty. That's because that hunger is rooted in our hungering for God, for a real and profound connection to the Divine. That desire for connection comes from deep in our bodies and souls. As theologian David Bentley Hart says, "Beauty crosses every boundary, traverses every series and so manifests the God who transcends every division." We are drawn to beauty as we are drawn to the Divine.

Closely linked to our hunger for beauty is our desire to create. Many of us, for whatever "good" reasons, give up being creative as we age. We've put away the PLAY-DOH, stopped making music with kazoos and waxed-paper-wrapped combs, quit telling each other fantastic stories and the like. We've stopped doing many of the things that gave us joy and hope and meaning when we were young.

These desires for beauty and creation are part of who we are— as creatures created in the image of our God. When we open Scripture, the first thing we see about God is a creative nature: "In the beginning God created the heavens and the earth" (Genesis 1:1 NIV). God brought order and beauty out of chaos. In that same way, a potter takes chaos in the form of clay and shapes it into something beautiful. Or a baker uses ingredients springing from the earth and its bounty and makes a cake. Or a supervisor sees the potential in the disparate talents of a company's workers and helps fashion them into an amazingly inventive team.

As writer Caroline C. Graveson, whom we quoted earlier in this book, said:

> There is a daily round for beauty as well as for goodness, a world of flowers and books and cinemas and clothes and manners as well as of mountains and masterpieces. . . . God is in all beauty, not only in the natural beauty of earth and sky, but in all fitness of language and rhythm, whether it describes a heavenly vision or a street fight, a Hamlet or a Falstaff, a philosophy or a joke: in all fitness of line and colour and shade, whether seen in the Sistine Madonna or a

child's knitted frock: in all fitness of sound and beat and measure, whether the result be Bach's Passion music or a nursery jingle. The quantity of God, so to speak, varies in the different examples, but His quality of beauty in fitness remains the same.

Seen that way, beauty is redemptive. Creativity, whether in the art studio or lived out in the workday world, invites us to participate in God's redemption of this world. God calls us to bring beauty and order from chaos, to bring glad tidings of great joy in every one of God's seasons.

We have been describing a creative, contemplative life, a deliberately thoughtful and purposeful life. As we touch, taste, see, hear and smell our way to God, our existence enlarges with new meaning. We are invited to collaborate with God in the art of creating, restoring and accomplishing good work in the world. It's an invitation we hear deep in our being.

Imagine what it would be like to live, sunup to sundown, looking for beauty, seeing yourself as a cocreator with God and keeping alert to your senses, allowing them to connect you with the Spirit's vocation in your world.

RHYTHMS THAT GROUND US

Living each day open to God through all five of our senses blurs the lines of what we traditionally think of as "sacred" or "spiritual." It reveals the sacrament of an ordinary day. Our senses, an extension of our bodies, teach us how to live incarnationally as the Spirit of Christ inhabits us and anoints our thoughts and responses to what they perceive. James Bryan Smith speaks about the healing of this common estrangement between the physical and spiritual:

Because we are sentient beings, everything we know about ourselves, other people, and our world comes through our senses. We are matter ourselves, so we perceive matter easily. This presents a huge problem when we start exploring the world of the spirit. We cannot smell, taste, touch, see, or hear the spiritual, so we hesitate to believe it is real. . . . The Holy Spirit helps us overcome this disunity by promoting the harmony of the physical and the spiritual. . . . The primary means that the Holy Spirit uses to heal this estrangement is our practice of spiritual disciplines. . . . The spiritual disciplines put our bodies in a place where God can work his goodness into us and bring harmony into our lives. And when our bodies and our spirits start to come back into harmony, we do away with categories. We easily move between religious and everyday activities, treating them as of equal value because God is present in both. . . . When our life is a "seamless garment," we are free to reveal God to the world.

Spiritual disciplines or rhythms ground us in life and meld the breach between the sacred and secular. When we fast and feel the rumble of hunger in our stomachs, our heart and body become one in our quest for God. When we sit in silence and worship God, our body and all our senses awaken to his holiness and presence. When we speak of Christ to another and hear our own voice telling our story, the words become spiritual and powerful. As we hold the Scriptures in our hands, feel the weight of this book we have come to love, touch its pages and listen to its message, we become aware of the Spirit speaking to us through it.

Though living as sentient Christians is a lifestyle, the habit is established and enhanced through daily rhythms and practices. As you continue your journey of growing as a spiritual sensate, consider the rituals of your daily life. Discover disciplines that unify your spirit and body. Experiment with new practices, ones that challenge you and strengthen your resolve to live life fully alive!

As a closing exercise, we invite you to write a prayer of commitment similar to the one at the beginning of the introduction to this book (p. 10). Work your way through each of your senses, bringing it to God as an offering, a means through which you come to him. Envision the world opening to you through your senses. Capture with words what you see, hear, feel, smell and taste.

Then, with your prayer deep in your soul, step out with eyes wide open, ears attuned, smelling the air around you, mouth watering for a fresh taste and skin sensitized to feel the wonder of God in each no-longer-ordinary day.

SENSORY EXERCISES

Additional Activities for Practicing a Sensuous Faith

DO THIRTY DAYS OF SENSING

Choose one of your physical senses and journal about that sense and how you experienced it and its spiritual dimensions each day. You may even want to set up a blog (they are free at sites such as blogger.com, wordpress.com and livejournal.com) and invite others to participate. For examples of how to do this, see Beth's "Peregrine Journey" (peregrinejourney.blogspot.com) or Brent's "Holy Ordinary" (holyordinary.blogspot.com).

CREATE A SPIRITUAL RECIPE BOOK

Think about your favorite recipes and what spiritual significance they have for you. Then bring them together in a booklet (if you use Microsoft Word you can download a free cookbook template). Present each recipe, where it came from (family, friends, favorite restaurant, etc.) and a brief explanation of its spiritual meaning to you. You could write a little thought about each one and its spiritual significance.

INVITE YOUR FAMILY TO DO A SENSE EXPERIMENT

Spend one day when you know your entire family (or a group of good friends) is going to be together just paying attention to your senses. Give everyone a small pad (like a four-by-eight-inch reporter's notebook, available at office supply stores). Write the name of one of the senses on the top of each page. Then have everyone pay attention to the various senses during the day and jot down, like a reporter, the who, what, where and why of each sense on their pads. Come together over a meal and share senses. Then ask them to tell where and how they sensed God in the senses they experienced.

BODY AND SENSES FOCUS

Take at least fifteen minutes and find a place in which to get comfortable. You can either sit or lie down—whatever works for you. Begin by taking some deep breaths and then just breathe normally. Pay attention to how your body feels—do you notice any tension? If you do, then think about relaxing that part of your body, releasing the tension to God. Next, focus your awareness on your senses. What do you hear? smell? feel? taste? see? Concentrate on the present moment and how you are experiencing God through your five senses.

CONSTRUCT A HOME ALTAR

While home altars are fairly new to Protestants, other Christians have been using them for centuries. Some are quite elaborate. But for our purpose, building a home altar can be as simple as dedicating some table space or using a shoebox or craft box as a place to pray. You can line the box with special paper or images and then place key items that will be conducive to contemplation for you. Use your senses—what sights, sounds, smells would connect you to God? You might want to use flower petals, holy water, candles, a small Bible, choose things that will enhance your personal prayer time.

ATTENTION-IN-LOVE EXERCISE

Look around you and answer the following questions:

- What do you see?
- What do you smell?

- What do you hear?
- What do you taste?
- What do you feel?

Now make a frame with your fingers. Look through it as you would a camera's viewfinder. Focus (pay attention) on a section of your view that you care about (love). Now . . .

- What do you see?
- What do you smell?
- What do you hear?
- What do you taste?
- What do you feel?

What difference(s) did you notice between the first experience and the second? Were you able to use both attention and love?

FIVE SENSES EXERCISE

Think concretely about a spiritual idea or feeling—like faith, grace or longing. Then, using that idea or feeling, finish the phrases below as concretely as possible. For example, take the word *faith* and insert it at the beginning so the phrases read:

- Faith smells like . . .
- Faith tastes like . . .
- Faith sounds like . . .
- Faith feels like . . .
- Faith looks like . . .

SENSING THE DAY

Instead of taking time out to focus on your senses, pay attention to them as they come to you throughout the day. For example, if you're eating something especially delightful, notice how it feels in your mouth, the aromas it releases, what it looks like in your hand as you bring it to your lips and so on. Or, while taking a walk, notice how your feet feel as they touch the ground and what the wind whisking by your face is like. What scents are in the air? What textures and feelings come to you through the soles of your shoes? Are your arms swinging freely, relaxed, or are you hunched and bound with tension? Pray your senses.

ASSEMBLE A FAITH MEAL

In a way similar to how Jews use Passover to tell their communal story of faith, plan a meal that tells your faith story. You could do this just for you or for your family or for your faith family (Sunday school class, small group, congregation). What foods would you choose? Would it be a breakfast, lunch or dinner? How would the meal progress—in what order would you serve your foods? Jews call the Passover meal "Seder," meaning "order." What would you call your faith meal?

HOLY SENSES FIELD TRIP

Take a day to visit some local congregations or other places you would consider sacred spaces. As you visit, look for the sights, smells, tastes, feelings and sounds of each place. Record them in your journal. What surprised you about the various places? What did they have in common? What was different? Which one felt, to you, like the place you most experienced God?

ART CONTEMPLATION

Visit an art museum or view art online, in your home or in this book, and choose an image to contemplate. Write in your journal about what stands out to you in the drawing, where your eyes are drawn and how this image speaks to you about that sense.

RESOURCES FOR AWAKENING YOUR SENSES

In addition to resources mentioned throughout the book and in the chapter endnotes, here are some additional books, CDs, websites and journals that we think are especially worth noting for their valuable insight into the art of awakening your senses to the wonder of God. While many of them are from an explicitly Christian perspective, some are not. We offer them for you to use at your discretion, hoping that you will use them wisely and well as they fit your needs. We thank our friends and artists from around the world who recommended many of these. They have enriched our experiences of God through our five senses.

ART, CREATIVITY AND SPIRITUALITY

Abbey of the Arts website: <www.AbbeyoftheArts.com>.

The Artist's Way: A Spiritual Path to Higher Creativity by Julia Cameron (New York: Tarcher/Putnam Books, 2002). Related website: <www.juliacameronlive.com>.

Awakening the Creative Spirit: Bringing the Arts to Spiritual Direction by Christine Valters Paintner and Betsey Beckman (Harrisburg, Penn.: Morehouse Publishing, 2010).

Free Play—Improvisation in Life and Art by Stephen Nachmanovitch (New York: Tarcher/Putnam Books, 1990).

God Is at Eye Level: Photography as a Healing Art by Jan Phillips (Wheaton, Ill.: Quest Books, 2000).

Image: Art, Faith, and Mystery website (Bimonthly journal, website, conferences and more): <www.imagejournal.org>.

Mind the Light: Learning to See with Spiritual Eyes by J. Brent Bill (Orleans, Mass.: Paraclete Press, 2006).

Picturing the Face of Jesus: Encountering Christ Through Art by Beth

Booram (Nashville: Abingdon, 2009).

Praying in Color and *Praying in Color: Kid's Edition* by Sybil MacBeth (Orleans, Mass.: Paraclete Press, 2007, 2009). Books and DVD.

The Quiet Eye: A Way of Looking at Pictures by Sylvia Shaw Judson (Washington, D.C.: Regnery, 1988).

Spirituality and Practice: Resources for Spiritual Journeys website: <www.spiritualityandpractice.com>.

Van Gogh and God—A Creative Spiritual Quest by Cliff Edwards (Chicago: Loyola Press, 1989).

Walking in This World by Julia Cameron (New York: Tarcher/Putnam, 2002).

HEARING AND VOICE

The Art of Spiritual Listening: Responding to God's Voice Amid the Noise of Life by Alice Fryling (Colorado Springs: Shaw, 2003).

Communing with Music: Practicing the Art of Conscious Listening by Matthew Cantello (Camarillo, Calif.: DeVorss & Company, 2004). Book and CD.

Lectio Divina: Renewing the Ancient Practice of Praying the Scriptures by M. Basil Pennington (New York: Crossroad, 1998).

Singing the Psalms: How to Chant in the Christian Contemplative Tradition by Cynthia Bourgeault (Boston: Shambhala Publications, 2006). Book and CD.

SEEING AND VISUAL ARTS

Christians in the Visual Arts (CIVA) website: <www.civa.org>.

Contemplative Vision: A Guide to Christian Art and Prayer by Juliet Benner (Downers Grove, Ill.: InterVarsity Press, 2010).

Drawing on the Right Side of the Brain: A Course in Enhancing Creativity and Artistic Confidence by Betty Edwards (New York: Tarcher, 1999). Related website: <www.drawright.com>.

The Little Book of Contemplative Photography by Howard Zehr (Intercourse, Penn.: Good Books, 2005).

Photography and the Art of Seeing: A Visual Perception Workshop for Film and Digital Photography by Freeman Patterson (Toronto: Key Porter Books, 2004).

Seeing the Word: Praying with Images from The Saint John's Bible website: <www.seeingtheword.org>.

Visual Journaling: Going Deeper Than Words by Barbara Ganim and Susan Fox (Wheaton, Ill.: Quest Books, 1999).

Windows into the Soul: Art as Spiritual Expression by Michael Sullivan (Harrisburg, Penn.: Morehouse Publishing, 2006).

TASTING AND SMELL

Bread, Body, and Spirit: Finding the Sacred in Food by Alice Peck (Woodstock, Vt.: Skylight Paths, 2008).

Heavenly Feasts: Memorable Meals from Monasteries, Abbeys, and Retreats by Marcia Kelly (Bloomington, Ind.: iUniverse, 2008).

Remembering Smell: A Memoir of Losing—and Discovering—the Primal Sense by Bonnie Blodgett (New York: Houghton Mifflin Harcourt, 2010).

The Spirit of Food: 34 Writers on Feasting and Fasting Toward God, edited by Leslie Leyland Fields (Eugene, Ore.: Wipf and Stock, 2010).

The Supper of the Lamb: A Culinary Reflection by Robert Farrar Capon (New York: Modern Library, 2002).

TOUCH, MOVEMENT AND DANCE

Body Prayer: The Posture of Intimacy with God by Doug Pagitt and Kathryn Prill (Colorado Springs: WaterBrook Press, 2005).

Centering in Pottery, Poetry, and the Person by M. C. Richards (San Francisco: Harper and Row, 1964).

Dance—The Sacred Art: The Joy of Movement as Spiritual Practice by Cynthia Winton-Henry (Woodstock, Vt.: Skylight Paths, 2009).

Danceprayer video by Carla DeSola (Mahwah, N.J.: Paulist Press).

Praying with Our Hands: 21 Practices of Embodied Prayer from the World's Spiritual Traditions by Jon M. Sweeney (Woodstock, Vt.: Skylight Paths, 2000).

Praying with the Body: Bringing the Psalms to Life by Roy DeLeon (Orleans, Mass.: Paraclete Press, 2009).

Sacred Dance Guild website: <www.sacreddanceguild.org>.

The Soulwork of Clay: A Hands-On Approach to Spirituality by Marjory Zoet Bankson (Woodstock, Vt.: Skylight Paths, 2008).

NOTES

p. 10 "That in the elements of earth": J. Phillip Newell, *Sounds of the Eternal: A Celtic Psalter* (Grand Rapids: Eerdmans, 2002), p. 42.

INTRODUCTION

p. 13 "We are over informed and under transformed": Dr. Terry Wardle of Ashland Theological Seminary at the Formational Prayer Seminar, June 2009, Ashland Seminary, Ashland, Ohio.

p. 14 "Now I was come up in spirit": George Fox, quoted in *Quaker Faith and Practice: Second Edition* (London: The Yearly Meeting of the Religious Society of Friends [Quakers] in Britain, 1995): 26:04.

p. 17 "All of life is sacramental; everything is a means of grace": Richard Rohr, as quoted by Dr. Terry Wardle at the Formational Prayer Seminar, June 2009.

p. 17 "daily round for beauty": Caroline C. Graveson, quoted in *Quaker Faith and Practice,* 21:28.

pp. 19-20 "Where can I *not* encounter the holy": Belden C. Lane, "The Ordinary as the Mask of the Holy," *The Christian Century,* October 3, 1984, p. 898.

TASTE

Introduction

p. 23 "Often we taste": Luci Shaw, "The Partaking," from *Accompanied by Angels: Poems of the Incarnation,* ed. Luci Shaw (Grand Rapids: Eerdmans, 2006), p. 63.

p. 24 "Take, eat: this is my Body, which is given for you": The (Online) Book of Common Prayer <www.bcponline.org/HE/ordhe .htm>.

p. 24   "The incarnate God is a potent embodiment": Mary Gordon, *Reading Jesus: A Writer's Encounter with the Gospels* (New York: Pantheon, 2009), p. 176.

p. 26   "A means of grace, as I use the phrase": Leland Ryken, "The Imagination as a Means of Grace," *Communiqué: A Quarterly Journal,* 4th Quarter, 1998 <www.communiquejournal.org/q4_printall.html>.

Keeping Kosher

p. 34   "Please, If it's not too late": Lyle Lovett, "Here I Am" (Studio City, Calif.: Michael H. Goldsen, Inc./Lyle Lovett, 1988).

Cravings

p. 42   Gary Thomas, in *Sacred Pathways:* Gary Thomas, *Sacred Pathways: Discover Your Soul's Path to God* (Grand Rapids: Zondervan, 2010).

Tasting Words

p. 52   "Contemplation leads to, or rather is an experience of, transcendence": William A. Barry and William J. Connolly, *The Practice of Spiritual Direction* (New York: HarperCollins, 1982), p. 50.

SEE

p. 58   Juliet Benner, in her book: Juliet Benner, *Contemplative Vision: A Guide to Christian Art and Prayer* (Downers Grove, Ill.: InterVarsity Press, 2010), p. 12.

Introduction

p. 59   "The real voyage of discovery": Marcel Proust, quoted in Jan Phillips, *Marry Your Muse: Making a Lasting Commitment to Your Creativity* (Wheaton, Ill.: Quest Books, 1997), p. 84.

p. 59   "Jesus is the Word made flesh": Sara Miles, *Jesus Freak: Feeding, Healing, Raising the Dead* (San Francisco: Jossey-Bass, 2010), p. 2.

p. 60   That wonder came back afresh after: Hugues de Montalembert, *Invisible: A Memoir* (New York: Atria, 2010), pp. 110-11.

p. 60   "You don't have enough attention to see what's around you": David Vestal, quoted in Steven J. Meyers, *On Seeing Nature* (Golden, Colo.: Fulcrum Group, 1986), p. 118.

p. 61   "As creatures who know the world through our senses": Christine Valters Paintner and Betsey Beckman, *Awakening the Creative Spirit: Bringing the Arts to Spiritual Direction* (Harrisburg, Penn.: Morehouse, 2010), p. 51.

p. 62   "There is nothing so secular that it cannot be sacred": Madeleine L'Engle, quoted in Phillips, *Marry Your Muse,* p. 15.

p. 62   "The most compelling images": Fazal Sheikh, quoted in Howard Zehr, *The Little Book of Contemplative Photography* (Intercourse, Penn.: Good Books, 2005), p. 18.

p. 63   "The eye with which I see God is the same": Meister Eckhart, *Meister Eckhart* (San Francisco: HarperSanFrancisco, 1957), p. 206.

p. 64   "wonder is the fuel which sustains vision": Meyers, *On Seeing Nature,* p. 98.

Reframe and Refocus

p. 71   "letting go of self is an essential precondition to real seeing": Freeman Patterson, *Photography and the Art of Seeing: A Visual Perception Workshop for Film and Digital Photography* (Toronto: Key Porter Books, 2004), p. 9.

p. 73   to behave "as if the old dominant ideas no longer exist": Ibid., p. 29.

p. 73   "happy accidents" that show us things in a new way: Ibid., p. 30.

p. 73   "Tell all the Truth but tell it slant": Anthony Hecht, "The Riddles of Emily Dickinson," in *Obbligati: Essays in Criticism* (New York: Atheneum, 1986), pp. 109, 111.

p. 73   J. B. Phillips wrote an important book: J. B. Phillips, *Your God Is Too Small* (New York: Touchstone, 1997).

p. 75   "My eyes find God everywhere, in every living thing": Jan Phillips, *God at Eye Level: Photography as a Healing Art* (Wheaton, Ill.: Quest Books, 2000), p. 8.

Reflecting Glory

p. 77   "Seeing alters the thing that is seen and transforms the seer": James Elkins, *The Object Stares Back: On the Nature of Seeing* (New York: Simon & Schuster, 1996), p. 11.

p. 79   "Nature was a mirror of the soul for St. Francis of Assisi." Richard Rohr, *In the Footsteps of Francis: Awakening to Creation,* webcast, <www.cacradicalgrace.org/Merchant2/merchantmvc?Screen=

PROD&Product_Code=ST-M-26&Category_Code=&Store_
Code=CFAAC>.

Going Off Grid

p. 81   "One looks, one longs, and the world comes in": Joseph Camp-
          bell, quoted in Jan Phillips, *God at Eye Level: Photography as a
          Healing Art* (Wheaton, Ill.: Quest Books, 2000), p. 55.
p. 82   "In the act of deeply seeing": Alex Grey, quoted in ibid., p. 7.

I See the Moon

p. 86   "I see the moon": Anonymous.
p. 87   "Something holds this all together": Rob Bell, *Velvet Elvis*
          (Grand Rapids: Zondervan, 2005), p. 76.

TOUCH

Introduction

pp. 95-96   The University of Minnesota staged an experiment: Allan and
            Barbara Pease, *The Definitive Book of Body Language* (New York:
            Bantam Dell, 2004), p. 104.

Textures

pp. 99-100 We all know the well-worn poem "Footprints": See <www
            .wowzone.com/fprints.htm>.

A Pile of Stones

p. 103   Just in case you are in the mood for white bean chicken chili,
          here is my recipe: <peregrinejourney.blogspot.com/2010/01/30-
          days-of-touching_12.html>.
p. 105   "every disability conceals a vocation, if only we can find it":
          Quoted in Sheldon Vanauken, *A Severe Mercy* (New York:
          Harper and Row, 1977), p. 146.

Touching Absence

p. 106   "Will the Lord reject us forever?": Psalm 77:7-8 from *The Psalms:
          A New Translation for Worship* (London: Collins, 1963).
p. 107   *Mother Teresa: Come Be My Light:* Brian Kolodiejchuk, ed.,
          Mother Teresa: Come Be My Light (New York: Doubleday,
          2007).

Feeling Your Prayers

p. 112   "While it is a crucial mistake to assume that churches": Eliza-
          beth O'Connor, *Journey Inward, Journey Outward* (New York:
          Harper & Row, 1968), p. ix.
p. 113   "As people on an inward journey, we are committed to growing
          in consciousness": Ibid., p. 13.
p. 113   "The goal we have been speaking of here is the one of getting
          our lives rooted in God": Ibid., p. 21.

Touching Jesus

p. 119   "If God is creator and we are made in God's image": Christine
          Valters Paintner and Betsey Beckman, *Awakening the Creative
          Spirit: Bringing the Arts to Spiritual Direction* (Harrisburg, Penn.:
          Morehouse, 2010), p. 13.
p. 120   "Oliver Twist: Please sir, I want some more": The Internet Movie
          Database, "Memorable Quotes for *Oliver!*" <www.imdb.com/
          title/tt0063385/quotes>.
p. 120   "In the stories of the risen Jesus": Sara Miles, *Jesus Freak: Feeding,
          Healing, Raising the Dead* (San Francisco: Jossey-Bass, 2010), p. 2.

HEAR

Introduction

p. 127   "Have you ever tried to spend a whole hour doing nothing but
          listening": Henri Nouwen, *Life of the Beloved: Spiritual Living in
          a Secular World* (New York: Crossroad, 2002), excerpt from In-
          ward/Outward daily meditation.

All the News

p. 143   "by making ourselves aware of the present moment of the uni-
          verse": "Praying the News," Spirituality & Practice: Resources
          for Spiritual Journeys website <www.spiritualityandpractice
          .com/links/index.php?id=15173>.
p. 143   "Lord of compassion and wisdom": "Praying the News," Bene-
          dictines of Heartsong Hermitage <www.benedictinesofheart
          songhermitage.org/catalog_2.html>.

Dinner Conversation

pp. 149-50   "Oh, how sweet and pleasant it is to the truly spiritual eye":

Isaac Pennington, quoted in *Quaker Faith and Practice: Second Edition* (London: The Yearly Meeting of the Religious Society of Friends [Quakers] in Britain, 1995), 27:13.

p. 152   "Art-making is somehow all at once a journey, *a communication, a modality*": Christine Valters Paintner and Betsey Beckman, *Awakening the Creative Spirit: Bringing the Arts to Spiritual Direction* (Harrisburg, Penn.: Morehouse, 2010), p. 5.

SMELL

Introduction

p. 158   "we learn to like and dislike various odors": "I Know What I Like: Understanding Odor Preferences," The Sense of Smell Institute online <www.senseofsmell.org/feature-detail.php?id=3>.

Smells Like . . . Worship

p. 162   "Now, can it be possible that in a handful of centuries": Mark Twain, "About Smells," About.com <classiclit.about.com/library/bl-etexts/mtwain/bl-mtwain-aboutsmells.htm>.

p. 163   "The incarnate God is a potent embodiment": Mary Gordon, *Reading Jesus: A Writer's Encounter with the Gospels* (New York: Pantheon, 2009), p. 176.

p. 164   "Knowledge of God was instilled in the believer who inhaled the scent of worship": Quoted in Robert Doran, review of *Scenting Salvation: Ancient Christianity and the Olfactory Imagination* by Susan Harvey, *Hugoye* 10, no. 1 (2007) <syrcom.cua.edu/Hugoye/Vol10No1/HV10N1PRDoran.html>.

Sea Salt and Midwest Mulberries

p. 171   "In simple trust like theirs who heard": John Greenleaf Whittier, "The Brewing of Soma," in *Selections from the Religious Poems of John Greenleaf Whittier* (Philadelphia: Tract Association of Friends, 1999), pp. 44-46.

p. 172   "All the way to heaven is heaven": Catherine of Sienna, quoted in Jan Phillips, *Marry Your Muse: Making a Lasting Commitment to Your Creativity* (Wheaton, Ill.: Quest Books, 1997), p. 106.

p. 174   "There's no place like home": The Internet Movie Database, "Memorable Quotes for *The Wizard of Oz*" <www.imdb.com/title/tt0032138/quotes>.

Wake Up and Smell the Communion

p. 180   "I'm on my second cup of coffee": Gordon Lightfoot, "Second
              Cup of Coffee" (Toronto: Moose Music, a division of Early
              Morning Productions Ltd., 1972).

p. 182   "The way to know God has always been by way of metaphor":
              Edward Lueders, quoted in Howard Zehr, *The Little Book of
              Contemplative Photography* (Intercourse, Penn.: Good Books,
              2005), p. 53.

p. 183   "we are called to openness, and sin is closing off ourselves from
              mystery": Pat Koehler, quoted in ibid., p. 35.

CONCLUSION

p. 186   "Beauty crosses every boundary, traverses every series": David
              Bentley Hart, *The Beauty of the Infinite: The Aesthetics of Chris-
              tian Truth* (Grand Rapids: Eerdmans, 2003), p. 21.

pp. 186-87   "There is a daily round for beauty as well as for goodness": Car-
              oline C. Graveson, quoted in *Quaker Faith and Practice: Second
              Edition* (London: The Yearly Meeting of the Religious Society of
              Friends [Quakers] in Britain, 1995), 21:28.

pp. 187-88   "Because we are sentient beings": James Bryan Smith with
              Lynda Graybeal, *A Spiritual Formation Workbook: Small Group
              Resources for Nurturing Christian Growth* (San Francisco: Harper-
              Collins, 1991), pp. 70-71.

PERMISSIONS

"Prayer for Awakening the Senses" by J. Phillip Newell, *Sounds of the Eternal: A Celtic Psalter* (Grand Rapids: Eerdmans, 2002) used by permission.

"The Partaking" by Luci Shaw, *Accompanied by Angels: Poems of the Incarnation* (Grand Rapids: Eerdmans, 2006) used by permission.

The illustrations *Thirsting for God (Psalm 63:1), Wonders Seen (Deuteronomy 10:21), The Work of God's Hands (Isaiah 64:8), Tell of God's Wonderful Deeds (Psalm 9:1),* and *An Aroma Pleasing (Leviticus 2:9)* created by Marcy Jean Stacey (marcystacey@gmail.com). Copyright 2010 Marcy Jean Stacey, J. Brent Bill, and Beth A. Booram. Used by permission.

All photographs by J. Brent Bill. Copyright 2011 J. Brent Bill. Used courtesy of the author.

ACKNOWLEDGMENTS

It is not an overstatement (or a bad pun) to say that we sensed the assistance and support of many people as we embarked on this project. From folks who attended our first workshops on this subject to others who contributed in unique ways, it is a joy to acknowledge them here.

We are grateful to InterVarsity Press for believing in this project and patiently nurturing its life. Cindy Bunch, our editor, honored our individual voices while pushing us, in her generous way, toward excellence. We wish to thank Jeff Crosby, associate publisher for sales and marketing, for his friendship and enthusiasm for this project.

Marcy Jean Stacey supplied the pencil drawings for the art meditations. Marcy is a Quaker artist who lives and makes art in southeastern Pennsylvania (marcystacey@gmail.com). Her finely detailed work and support of this project are deeply appreciated.

Our families have been a formative influence in teaching us how to live as sensory beings at home with them in this world.

Brent is grateful to Nancy for her support of his writing and for giving him the space and time to be creative, especially when he knows she'd rather be working in the garden or prairie than reading the same pieces over and over again. She's also a good proofreader and wise critic.

Beth is grateful for David—an artist, poet and beautiful soulmate—who is patient and supportive as she writes away. She is thankful, as well, for her adult kids—Britt, Brandt and Laura (and grandson Eli!), Bri and Brooke—for their genuine interest and constant encouragement.

For friends who grace our lives and help us taste the richness of relationship, we are indebted. Brent wishes to thank Marcy Jean Stacey, Aaron Spiegel, Nancy Armstrong and Tim Shapiro for their friendship and support of his writing and photography. Brent is also grateful to the good people at Pendle Hill, a Quaker conference center in Wallingford, Pennsylvania, for providing him a place to write a substantial portion of this book.

Beth is grateful for Tim and Mary, Nate and Megan, Steve and Samantha—her true church and dearest companions. For a host of others who bless her life with the gift of presence and influence: Ann, Jan, Sandee, Pam, Phil and Jim. Beth also wishes to thank Dave and Jody Nixon for their hospitality during her writing retreats at the convent of Sustainable Faith.

CONNECTING WITH THE AUTHORS

We have created a website to help you continue your journey into the senses: awakenyoursenses.us.

You can also email us through the site:

- brentbill@awakenyoursenses.us
- bethbooram@awakenyoursenses.us

Our twitter feed is http://twitter.com/#!/WakenYourSenses. Also, look for our Facebook page for *Awaken Your Senses*.

ABOUT J. BRENT BILL

In addition to his ministry of writing, Brent also enjoys a ministry of leading workshops and speaking. Some of his most popular workshops are

- Awaken Your Senses (with Beth Booram)
- The Sacred Compass: Spiritual Practices for Discernment
- Being Quiet: The Practice of Holy Silence
- Writing from the Heart: Telling Your Soul's Stories

If you would like more information about Brent's writing or his spirituality workshops and retreats, or would like to contact him about other speaking engagements, you can reach him through his website at www.brentbill.com or via e-mail at brentbil@brent bill.com. You can read new material and see photography by Brent at holyordinary.blogspot.com.

ABOUT BETH A. BOORAM

Beth Booram has been a lifelong vocational minister in parachurch settings as well as mainline and nondenominational churches. She is a spiritual director and healing prayer practitioner, as well as a congregational consultant. Beth speaks around the country at conferences and retreats on topics of spiritual life and Christian leadership. Some of her topics include

- Awaken Your Senses (with Brent Bill)

- The Wide Open Spaces of God: A Journey with God Through the Landscapes of Life

- Picturing the Face of Jesus: Encountering Christ Through Art

- Using Experientials in Training and Teaching

If you would like more information about Beth's writing or her workshops and retreats, or would like to contact her about other speaking engagements, you can reach Beth through her website at www.bethbooram.org or via e-mail at bethbooram@sbcglobal.net. You can read her most current thoughts at peregrinejourney.blog spot.com.